Η ΖΩΗ ΜΑΣ
(Our Life)

Η ΖΩΗ ΜΑΣ
(Our Life)

by

Louis Garbis

Copyright © 2022, Louis Garbis

All rights reserved. Printed in the U.S.A.

No part of this publication may be reproduced or transmitted in any form or by any means, electronic or mechanical, including photocopy, recording or any information storage and retrieval system now known or to be invented, without permission in writing from the publisher, except by a reviewer who wishes to quote brief passages in connection with a review written for inclusion
in a magazine, newspaper or broadcast.

Quantity Purchases:
Companies, professional groups, clubs, and other organizations may qualify for special terms when ordering quantities of this title.
For information, email info@ebooks2go.net,
or call (847) 598-1150 ext. 4141.
www.ebooks2go.net

Published in the United States by eBooks2go, Inc.
1827 Walden Office Square, Suite 260, Schaumburg, IL 60173

ISBN: 978-1-5457-5647-8 (Paperback)
ISBN: 978-1-5457-5648-5 (Hardcover)

Library of Congress Cataloging in Publication

Contents

The Diogenes Syndrome ix

Acknowledgement. xi

Dedication xiii

Introduction xv

Chapter 1   The Gerasimos and Arsinoi
Garbis Family 1
    Family Origins 5

Chapter 2   My Siblings 9
    Andoni (Tony): The Shepherd Boy. 9
    Andoni: The Produce Merchant 10
    Kostadina (Dina) 12
    Dionisios (Denny) 14
    Eleftherios (Ted) 18
    Kathy 22
    Vasilios (Bill) of Greece 26
    Bill of America 29

Chapter 3   Childhood Memories 37
    Zografia. 45
    The Planned Agreement to Adopt 52

**Chapter 4 Commentaries of Relevant and Socially
        Impactful Topics** **63**

    A Comparison of the Greek and American Civil Wars 63

    The disturbing Issue of Slavery in America. 64

    The plight of the Indigenous Americans 65

    An Overview of Communism versus Democracy 67

    A Brief Overview of Greece's
Contribution to WWII 69

    Final comments on Greece's Contributions
during WWII. 72

    A special Thank you to a Special Mentor 74

    May School. 77

    Return to Socrates 77

    Longfellow Grammar School. 80

    Oak Park High 81

    University of Illinois, Chicago 83

    Career in Risk Management and Insurance. 84

    General Observations of Greeks in Foreign Lands. 86

Chapter 5 The 1996 Brotherly Excursion to Kefalonia. 87

    A Man of Honor 87

    A night to Remember—or Not. 88

Chapter 6 Relatives **93**

    Gerasimos (Father) 93

    A Father-and-Son Spiritual Moment 96

    Arsinoe (Mother) 97

    Family Attributes 98

    Athanasios And Reginna 100

    Respect and Honor the Ancestors 102

Anastasia (Tasia) Kourouklis 104

Pavlatae 107

Vasilios Kourouklis 111

Heartfelt Tribute to Dickie, Our Best and
Dearest Friend 117

Chapter 7   Leaving for America 119

Kedzie and Washington 121

Congress and Van Buren 122

Oak Park 123

Chapter 8   Epilogue 127

Appendix A: Battle of Mezenkert-a Brief Synopsis 131

Appendix B: Garbis Family Tree 135

Appendix C: Family Photos 139

The Diogenes Syndrome

There was a man named Diogenes who lived around 300 BC. He was considered a sophist and highly respected by many, to the extent he became renowned throughout the Hellenic World, including Alexander the Great.

Diogenes and his acolytes were called by other fellow citizens « Σκύλο ανθρώποι» (dog people). This is because they covered their privates with only a loincloth. Most telling, they behaved like dogs in relieving themselves in public, including other well-known canine characteristics and proclivities.

As the story goes, on one bright, sunny afternoon, Diogenes was spotted in his normal attire holding a lighted lamp, walking the streets and searching for someone or something.

A bemused citizen asked the philosopher, "Diogenes, what in Zeus's name are you doing?"

Diogenes answered in a solemn tone, "I am looking for an honest man".

And like the Diogenes of old, I am looking for my family's past.

Acknowledgement

A big thank you to,

To my niece Anastasia Verdone for providing the voluminous number of family photos that visualized the telling of our family story.

To my cousin, Nikki Proutsos who shared the legal records of our grandparent's genealogy and allowed us to obtain a better understanding of who came before us.

To my parents and siblings who shared their personal stories with their youngest child, who thought them significant benefit to their decedents and worth telling.

To my wife Phyllis who found me a wonderful publisher eBooks2go and made my task much easier.

Dedication

To the loving family I was blessed to be born in and all our recent ancestors—much of the good that I am and much of what I accomplished I owe to them. They provided the history and the genes. All the bad I owe to my naivety and the impulsive foolishness and self-righteous boldness of my youth. For my indiscretions, I apologize to our ancestors and to our descendants.

To our heroes and ancestors of antiquity and their profound wisdom, heroism, curiosity, and logic. These attributes and a great deal of deep, complex thinking took them on a never-ending journey to identify physical and metaphysical theories and concepts in search of truth, as well as their place in their surroundings and in the universe.

They greatly influenced global thought and behavior, especially Western Civilization—Homer, Aristotle, Leonidas, Themistocles, Odysseus, Alexander the Great, and the polymath Eratosthenes, who around 240 BC opined that the Earth was round and came accurately close in measuring its circumference (24,662 versus the actual 24,901 miles). More than one ancient Greek deduced that the Earth was round, including another polymath, Aristotle. Finally, we cannot forget to pay homage to a vital hero of the 1821 struggle for Greek independence, Athanasios Diakos, and many more too numerous to name!

To our heroes of World War II, who were the first of the Allies to win battles against the Axis powers (Germany and Italy). Until then, the Axis powers in Europe were an unstoppable, well-oiled juggernaut that tore through Europe like a machine harvesting wheat. Additional comments on this topic, including the American and Greek Civil War, communism versus democracy, and the plight of the Native Americans are discussed in chapter 4 of this book.

To my wonderful wife, Phyllis, for her tolerance, forgiving ways and extreme patience. In many ways, you gave and continue to provide me life, strength, and comfort. Most of all, for giving me three beautiful children. As a Don Williams country song says, "Till the rivers all are dry, till the Sun falls from the sky, till life on Earth is through, I will be needing you."

To Katerina, Jeramiah, and George—despite a father who was rarely around during your youth, you continue and never cease to make me proud of the people you have become. Thank you! I can only imagine the heights you will achieve in your long, bountiful, and industrious lives. I thank the Almighty for allowing me the privilege to be your father. Be assured, much of what I do or ever did, you and your mother were the primary motivation, as well as our ancestors, to whom we owe everything. I hope you continue the gift of history that they bestowed upon us. It is my hope and wish that you and your descendants continue to write our story for ages and ages to come! «Νυν και είναι και εις τους αιώνες των αιώνων αμήν»

With unconditional love to all,
Ilias G. Garbis

Introduction

Many Americans, and most people around the world, live an ephemeral life. Live for today. Once today passes, in time, it is readily forgotten. With recent interest in genealogy and DNA testing, it is reasonable to assume there exists significant curiosity about our past. For some of us, it is imperative we learn as much as possible about our family history. In doing so, we become more complete and more at peace with our inner selves. Who were our ancestors? Do we have similarities? Do we share certain behaviors? If there are undesirable or dangerous tendencies, can we learn from the past so as not to repeat it? If there is good in our past, can we use it to empower ourselves to strive for even greater heights of success? Are there important health issues we need to address?

For some, the interest is more of a novelty, without a serious attempt to learn about one's ancestral roots. I would infer that if one were to ask one hundred people if they knew their grandparents, the expected result would be close to or 100 percent. If one were to ask them who their great-grandparents were, many would have a difficult time remembering their names, let alone fundamental facts about their lives. If one were to extrapolate to earlier generations, for the majority, remembering names, ages, eras, and other significant facts would be an unsurmountable task. If this perception is accurate, that would be a huge loss for all involved, especially our ancestors, as their history would be forgotten, thus robbing us of key information that would empower us to live our lives in an improved and constructive manner.

Regarding health, we know that our family, probably the Garbis side, needs to be weary of penicillin, or a derivative, as it may prove lethal. It almost killed my brother Bill. A drug, Ceclor, which included a derivative of penicillin, gave me hives and significant discomfort. The harsh reactions were mitigated by steroids and lasted for over six long and vexing months!

Dust mites, mold, and preservatives cause allergic reactions in which my nasal cavities inflame and completely close. This reaction would cause me to wake up at various hours of the night. I would pace the room until the tension passed, and my breathing stabilized. This agonizing nightly routine occurred on a regular basis—about six-plus months—until a solution was found.

We first tore up all our floor carpeting and replaced it with wood flooring. And after trying allergy shots and numerous allergy sprays, which proved ineffective, we identified an allergy spray, Rhinocort. It did not totally erase the allergic reactions, but it significantly mitigated them, allowing me to enjoy a "reasonable" amount of sleep. Adding the nasal strip Breathe Right was an integral component to being able to breathe through my nose with hardly any obstruction. It is a shame it took me and my doctors so long to figure it out.

Note that I am only addressing the *family loss* and potential costs that may be attributed to ignorance of these and other maladies, medical or mental, and not the broader and exponentially larger loss to our society. Bottom line: the more we know of our family history, the more likely we are to enjoy fulfilling, purposeful lives.

It is an axiom of life that "knowledge is power, and education is the foundation of our society." Key interests of mine are history, natural science, and astronomy. I was not born with a high intellect and IQ. But I had and still have an unquenchable thirst to learn pretty much anything and everything that makes up this world and universe. I realize that irrespective of how much I read and learn, to paraphrase Socrates's famous observation, "I know nothing." But still, to us mortals, learning and education are meaningful and essential in so many obvious ways. I always had—and hopefully will always have—a healthy curiosity about life and my surroundings and will continue to ask, "Why?" until the day I die.

Because of my insatiable curiosity and an unyielding thirst for knowledge, my interests have resulted in sleepless nights and embarrassing forgetfulness—sometimes to a fault. But to me, it is worth all this and more. On the plus side, I have learned many life lessons.

A key one I remind friends and family is that small positive steps, in time, will take a person on a long and rewarding path. I have learned mistakes are not mistakes if they are learned from and not repeated. Mistakes are then transformed into constructive and empowering experiences.

The purpose of this book is to introduce our family to our descendants with a primary focus on our life in Kefalonia, Greece—their errors, idiosyncrasies, their good, and their bad. Despite living in extreme poverty during the difficult times of World War II, the Greek Civil War, and the 1953 earthquake that was centered by Kefalonia, they persevered. You will find them human and imperfect, supportive of each other, proud, a loving and caring family. Most took the Old-World hardships with them to the New World and turned them into positive experiences and unconditional successes. They did not allow their lack of education and their severe hardships to define them. They were intrepid in every sense of the word. They made their ancestors proud. They make us, their descendants, proud.

Intermittent and near the end of this family's journey, are abbreviated discussions relative to our life in America. It is my hope and wish that by writing this book our descendants will learn of our recent history, including our strengths and weakness. It is also my hope they will use this information as foundational in getting to know our ancestors. They were not perfect, but nobody is. But as you will discover, they were fine, honorable people who made a positive difference to all those they came across and to their families.

Furthermore, the goal of humanity is to learn from their errors in life's myriad winding paths to strive for the unreachable-perfection! It is recognized that humankind can never achieve perfection, but the ongoing struggle to get there will continuously improve us. Also, in learning of our past, we might find commonalities and a sense of belonging. Most important, it should empower us in many positive and constructive ways.

I want our descendants, including nieces and nephews, to know they were and are unconditionally loved, appreciated, and respected. That is our way; that is the only way. It is my hope they take pride in their origins, never forgetting who we were or where we came from.

CHAPTER 1

The Gerasimos and Arsinoi Garbis Family

My baptismal name is Ilias G. Garbis. The *G*, *gamma* in Greek, is the initial of my father's first name, Gerasimos. The *G* here is for Gerasimou. The *mou* states that I am a descendant of Gerasimos. For Greeks, it is customary for a descendant to indicate his or her father's first name as a middle initial. I was advised by the late Father Triantafilis, a prior protopresbyter of the Saint Nectarios Greek Orthodox Church, Palatine, Illinois, that the name *Gerasimos* means "strong-willed." This makes sense, since *geros* is defined as "strong" in Greek.

Father Triantafilis was the priest who helped me find my way back to a more comfortable acceptance of religion. I do not believe he was popular with some of the churchgoers, as his approach was "old school." On rare occasions, those who, in his opinion, did not follow church etiquette could expect a "gentle" reprimand. To be fair, he had just as many parishioners who respected and adhered to his church decorum. I was one of them. Whether strict, conservative, or liberal, I look for sincerity and intent. In both categories, Father Triantafilis easily met the threshold. He was genuine.

I had the pleasure of being a member of the Saint Nectarios Parish Council in the late 1980s for a four-year stint. In that time, he, I, and other members of the council made constructive contributions that benefited the parish and its parishioners. I also gained several lifelong friends. One of them was Father Triantafilis.

Our father was born on January 20, 1916, to Nikolaos and Ekaterini Garbis. He was the fourth of nine children: Eleni, Antelini, Dionisios, Gerasimos, Athanasios, Spiros, Gerasimoula, Georgeos, and Angeliki. A copy of our family tree is included in this book's appendix. It is a beginning, not an ending. It still requires additional work to make it more substantive, more complete. It will also require our descendant's input to continue to update and refine our family's history.

Their youngest offspring, Angeliki, I am told was not only a natural beauty but had a beautiful heart. She had a caring disposition and a willingness to sacrifice herself for a loved one. The one example I am aware of is when my brother Andoni (Tony) was a baby and thought to be stricken with a serious and highly contagious disease, likely tuberculosis.

Our mother warned Angeliki to not hold Andoni, as she might catch this virulent disease and die. She replied, "Better me than my Andoni." Sadly, she got her wish. She passed away on May 6, 1945, at the age of twenty, roughly three years after she had made that comment. I do not know the cause of death. Based on historical context, the likely candidate was tuberculosis. A potential cure for this disease was identified in 1943 by Selman Walksman. After refinements and clinical trials, it was successfully administered to patients in November 1949.

Our mother, Arsinoe, was born on December 6, 1906, to Panagiotis and Anastasia Kourouklis. She had two brothers: Christopher and Vasilios. Christopher was the oldest, and my mother was the youngest. I met Christopher and his family for the first time when I visited Greece in 1972. I found him kind and hospitable, as was his family. In fact, I was so sufficiently impressed with his kind demeanor that I named my second child Christopher Jeramiah, in his and my father's honor. When my father passed, I missed him and felt regret for not naming him just Gerasimos, which was customary for Greeks. As a result, I always call him Gerasimos or J. J likes and uses both names but uses Christopher as his first name in most of his communications.

I was born on November 18, 1950, in Vlahata, in the municipality of Omalon, Kefalonia, Greece. I was the seventh and last child of our mother, Arsinoe, and the fifth child of our father. I was born with curly red hair. Because I would cry when my mother combed my hair, she finally had enough of my complaints and shaved my head. Head shavings were common in that era for Greek boys. Our mother and grandmother Anastasia were also born with red hair, which in time turned brown. We have this in common. No one else in our family has that distinction.

Our father was from the same village as our mother—Frangata. He was ten years younger. Based on her wedding picture, she was very beautiful and thin. Regrettably, that photograph has been lost and to date has not been found. Our father was smart, quick-witted, and a good judge of character. He was also a fast runner, which earned him the nickname "Koukayiaki," after a fast runner who preceded him who was also a resident of Frangata. As the pages that follow suggest, he was also a tough guy and adapted well to the difficult times of the 1940s.

Our mother married my father roughly two years after her first husband's sudden death in Panama. He was probably twenty-one, and she was thirty-one. Our father moved to Vlahata, where our mother lived in her deceased husband's house. This was a two-story building with four bedrooms and stairs on both sides that were located outside. The house had front and back balconies and a decent-sized veranda. The main structure was for sleeping. A dining room existed for special occasions and guests. A second smaller structure existed nearby, which was the kitchen. It was used for cooking and day-to-day eating. The third and final structure was the outhouse. Based on what I have gathered from my siblings, it was one of the better homes in the village.

Vlahata is where we were all born and lived until we departed for America. Although I was about three months short of three years of age, I recall that after the earthquake of 1953, only the foundations were visible, clearly identifying the location of the razed house. Much later in life, I learned the main house was still standing after the earthquake. But due to the resulting significant structural damage, it was too dangerous to continue to live in the house. Hence the decision was made to have it torn down. After it was dismantled, materials were given to our brother-in-law, Toto (Erotokritos), and Dina when they were married as part of her dowry. I'm not clear on the total dowry arrangement. The remaining materials from the house were used to erect a shack so the family would have a "roof" over its head.

My two eldest siblings' (Dina and Denny) father, Panagiotis Markadonatos, was killed in Panama in the mid-1930s. It is my understanding that Dina was about two, and Denny was only few months old. His demise and the circumstances surrounding his death are discussed in the section titled "Vasilios Kourouklis." Out of respect for the deceased, our father did not legally adopt Denny or Dina. He thought Dina and Denny should carry the last name of their blood father (Markadonatos). From all that I have heard, he was a good person, a family man, and a good provider for his family.

I'm not certain if our father's decision caused Denny issues growing up since the rest of us carried the surname Garbis, and Denny's and Dina's surname was Markadonatos. Sometimes there is just no good solution—damned if you do, and damned if you don't. Irrespective, there was, is, and will always be unconditional love for all. In fact, I did not comprehend that Dina and Denny were half-blood siblings until my teens. Even then, I never thought much about it. It was completely irrelevant!

When our father also became Dina's and Denny's father, from all I saw and recall, he treated both like all his children—equally, if not better. But an incident occurred when Denny was about fourteen years of age that is worth mentioning. He was asked to pick up thirty drachmas from someone who owed our father this amount for work performed. In the mid-1940s, from an exchange rate standpoint, thirty drachmas was much less than thirty dollars. But so was the cost of goods in a shattered Greek economy, ruined by World War II and the Greek Civil War, which produced huge unemployment and starvation.

These funds were essential to the family. It was Christmas, one of the holiest days of the year. The funds would allow us to obtain meat and other holiday-related consumables to properly celebrate this holy time of the year. Unlike most of the world, in our little town of Vlahata and most of Greece, Christmas was a small and private celebration to commemorate the birth of our Savior, Jesus of Nazareth. No Christmas parties, no gift-giving, no bright lights. It was strictly about celebrating this holy event and survival. But to us, with all our family together, for one evening it felt like heaven.

Denny went on his bike and picked up the funds. On his return trip, he stopped at a nearby coffee shop, about a mile away from the house, played cards, probably with seasoned gamblers, and lost all the money. Without these funds, if another source was not identified, the family would go hungry, and that was not an option.

When Denny finally came home, he took a knife, gave it to our father, and asked him to kill him. Our father, of course, would have none of that talk. But he did, I hope, discipline Denny for his irresponsible behavior. Starvation and death by emaciation were not rare. In fact, history tells us that starvation in that era was a bit too common, especially on a national scale. Clearly, Denny's behavior in our time of need was inexcusable. It could have placed the family in a precarious position. A potential solution was identified. It will be discussed in the "Vasilios Kourouklis" section.

As a matter of record, when Greece finally fell to the Germans during World War II, German leadership directed the local generals to make certain that most of the food produced was taken from the conquered peoples—by force, if necessary—so the German soldiers would be well fed. Any excess would be sent to their forces in North Africa or where food supplies were needed to help their war effort. The fate and plight of the locals was not a serious concern of the occupier.

With this draconian directive, history suggests over one hundred thousand citizens died of starvation in just the first year alone. Many were city dwellers or poor folk in the villages who had little or no farming or livestock to help them survive. We fell into the latter category. A couple of important variables allowed us to survive. One was that steady local work was available for the eldest two brothers and our father. All took jobs when and where they could. Another key contributor was Grandmother Anastasia, who is discussed in more detail later in this book. This directive was surprising, since the Germans were mostly amicable and respected the Greeks due to their history and contributions to the Western civilization. But as the adage suggests, "In love and war, anything goes."

Denny's love of cards was an ominous precursor of things to come. On the plus side, Denny worked hard to help the family get by during those hard and difficult times. Despite his gambling habit, it was almost impossible not to like our eldest brother. Denny was smart, mentally quick, good-hearted, personable, and generous to a fault. He also had an excellent singing voice.

Family Origins

I know very little of our family's origins. Below is a brief summary of what I have learned on the Garbis side:

- Our father's origins appear to be from Italy. If so, I surmise the Garbises migrated to Kefalonia around the 1700s, plus or minus one hundred years. That time frame is liberally deduced and is based on what little information I have been able to gather as to when Venice first occupied Kefalonia. That occurred in the early 1500s and lasted until 1797.
- There were at least three brothers who migrated to Kefalonia. I have not yet ascertained if they came with wives and children. Their names were Yacomo (I assume a derivation of John), Ricardo, and George. I believe these three had the clan name Liguris. At least, that is what my father's clan was called—Liguris, Ligurithes, Liguraieee. I do not believe this nickname is of Greek origin. Trying to determine where the Garbises came from, I did a Google search that was uneventful. Except for one thing: The municipality where Genoa is located is called Liguria. It does not seem a stretch to deduce that we were called "liguraieee," as perhaps that was where the Garbis originally came from. For Example, in America, I have often been called by Americans the "Greek," by Greeks in America "Kefaloniti," and when I am in Kefalonia "American." To make things a bit more interesting, there is a town near Genoa called Garbarino. In pictures, it appears old, with very few occupants, if any. Still, this may be a bit of a stretch. Only by visiting Genoa and looking at birth certificates starting from the fifteenth, sixteenth, seventeenth, and early eighteenth centuries will it be possible to provide a more accurate time frame and family tree.
- Yacomo was probably the oldest of the brothers. I say this because as you enter Frangata, the plot of land on the right side, as soon as you reach the town line, is called Jacomata (Jacomo's land). We know that Saint Gerasimos, our patron saint, was near what is called Frangata in or around the late 1580s. I have not identified when exactly Frangata was first settled or when the Garbis migration to Frangata began.
- A very good uncle who liked to dabble in our origins, Athanasios Garbis, once shared with me that he thought our father's family was from the Ricardo tree, and we were nicknamed "Hardaiee." He suggested this nickname meant that we are known to be loud. I hate to admit this—we can be loud, yours truly included. Still, the foundation of our family is yet to be identified.

There is much I need to find out about the missing years. For example, what motivated the brothers to migrate to Kefalonia? My guess is that when Venice became the dominant power in the Adriatic and the Mediterranean Sea, it is reasonable to assume they invited fellow Italians looking to inhabit this newly acquired territory, with a promise of free land, power, and more. Venice's motivation was obvious. It would allow them better control of their newly occupied land. Kefalonia became a vassal of Venice from 1500 until 1797. It became a vassal because Byzantium was fighting the Bulgars and wanted Venice to manage its Ionian interests. In or around 1797, Napoleon Bonaparte dissolved Venice, and for a brief period after 1797 Kefalonia was ruled by France, then overseen by Russia, and then subsequently became a protectorate of England from 1815 until 1864.

In 1864 England, France, and Russia signed the Treaty of London, pledging the transfer of sovereignty to Greece. The British intention was to bolster the reign of King George I of Greece. He was of Danish descent, and all three countries benefited via marriages from this move. The biggest gain was by Greece, since the Ionian Islands were once again unified with their motherland.

Frangata can be interpreted as "the village of the Francs," implying French origins. This is just a conjecture, but it does not seem unreasonable, as I have not been able to identify a better explanation as to how Frangata received its name. Not to complicate matters, I subsequently read in more than one reference that Greeks would call anyone from the west "Frangee." Probably from the Norman-Frankish Crusades that passed through Greece to fight the Saracens. Perhaps a French knight decided to make that village his home and gave it this name. This is strictly a theory and has yet to be proven.

Irrespective of the above comments, many of the surnames from Frangata have a foreign touch and imply Italian roots. For example, one of our close family friend's last name was Maraveyias, which in Italian and Spanish is *maravioso*, or "marvelous." Another name is Fabiotos. I surmise that Fabioano or something similar was the original name, and the "atos" probably added to make it easier to assimilate into Hellenism.

In America, when I became an adult, my father shared that in Frangata and the neighboring town, Valtsamata, men did not die of old age.

He implied that they died from vendettas. I suppose with this revelation we can forget about the Franks and welcome the Paisanos! Thankfully, that description of foreigners no longer applies. *Xenos*, which translates to "foreigner," is the now the governing definition for all peoples who are not of Greek origin.

My paternal grandparents were Nikolaos Garbis, and my grandmother was Ekaterini (kakia) who was a Pavlotos prior to her marriage. As previously noted, they had five sons and four daughters who lived to adulthood. In order of birth: Eleni, Antelini, Dionisis, Gerasimos, Athanasios, Spiro, and Georgos. Regrettably, I know even less about my grandmother's family origins. I do know that my grandmother Anastasias's maiden name was Mesolouras. That is all I know and next to nothing about my maternal grandfather except that he died young.

For the record, the surname *Garbis* suggests Armenian origin. Armenians in America have stopped me more than once who thought I was Armenian and called me brother. When I advised I was Greek, they were shocked by this revelation. That discussion occurred on the Eisenhower (I-290), when I was in my late twenties. Thank God there was no traffic when they flagged me down!

I like my Armenian friends, but when the occasion arises I make it clear to all who are curious of my ethnicity that, although my mind is more American in perception and thought, my soul will always be Greek, with a heavy bias toward the historical and ancient Greeks. Whether in science, theoretics, philosophy, problem-solving, courage, or sacrifice, with their amazing accomplishments, they defined the glory that *was* Greece. Throughout their time on Earth, they sculpted a path vivid and resounding that they made sure, that even the deaf among us would hear them, be empowered by them, and never forget them! In my old age, even if I forget who I am, I do not believe I will ever forget those who came before me and what that means to us of Hellenic origin.

CHAPTER 2

My Siblings

My siblings and I, in order of birth, are as follows:

- Kostandina (Dina)—12/04/1934; died on 11/24/2019 of stage four kidney failure; age eighty-five.
- Dionisios (Denny)—4/25/1936; died on 5/29/2001; deceased due to a heart condition at sixty-five years old.
- Andonis (Tony)—10/09/1939; died on 12/04/2019; he was diagnosed with cancer. A clinical trial drug that was utilized in the second stage appeared to have severely damaged key parts of his internal organs. This news was highly unexpected, and his death occurred within forty days from the time of the drug's reaction. He was eighty.
- Eleftherios (Ted) 81—4/15/1941
- Ekaterini (Kathy) 79—2/12/1943
- Vasilios (Bill)—01/01/1946; died in 10/21/2001; passed at fifty-five years old; the cause of Bill's death was a ruptured heart artery.
- Ilias (Louis) 72—11/18/1950

Below is an overview of the jobs I am aware that Tony, as a young lad, undertook as our family and most of Greece suffered from hunger and starvation.

Andoni (Tony): The Shepherd Boy

Tony grew up in the era of World War II (1940–1945) and the Greek Civil War (1943–1944; 1946–1949). He had it tougher than most in his youth.

Because of his stature and measured demeanor that exuded excellence, responsibility, and trust, he was in demand by local employers. Even as a youth, he worked hard and long for the family, probably since the age of ten.

Our father's friend Panagis Hionis had a herd of goats and was looking for a shepherd boy to watch and take them to graze. Our father volunteered Andoni for that job. The stable and the pastures were somewhere on Mount Ainos. This mountain, at its peak, is roughly a 5,341-feet elevation from sea level. I'm not certain how high or how far Tony took the herd.

I am certain that Andoni was unable to come home and lived and worked with little if any interaction with family or people. It must have been lonely for him. But he never complained and worked tirelessly to help feed a hungry family. The only person who interacted with him, on occasion, was the owner of the herd.

After about two months, my father visited his beloved son. Even at a young age, Andoni was not one to complain. After seeing his son worn from loneliness and a lack of human interaction, our father was heartbroken. He said to him, "Antoni mou, you are coming back with me today. We are all starving in the village, but if we starve, we shall all starve to death together!" And they went home together. Knowing my father, he must have had moist eyes, sad with a feeling of remorse as he spoke to his beloved son. As a father myself, I, too, empathize, and feel his pain.

Andoni: The Produce Merchant

Vlahata is about a half mile from the sea and warm enough to grow fruits like oranges. At lower levels, one can even grow bananas. After returning to the village, at about the age of eleven or twelve, my father assigned Andoni the job of filling two large handmade barrels with oranges, and with our donkey, Kapsoula, he walked up the mountain to Frangata, our parents' village of birth. In Frangata, where everyone knew our parents, and many relatives and friends lived there, Andoni found willing customers. That is because oranges cannot be grown at Frangata's higher altitude, which is roughly thirty-five-hundred-plus feet above sea level. Near the upper section of the village, Vlahata approximates about seven hundred feet above sea level.

These trips to Frangata were performed three times a week, inclusive of cold days, snow days, rainy days, and most any kind of days. Andoni would commence his journey by walking with Kapsoula next to him about fifteen miles uphill at three in the morning. He would charge five drachmas for six oranges. On cold days, out of pity and impressed with this young man's toughness, friends of my parents would occasionally invite him to stop in for a hot tea to warm up before continuing the long journey to Frangata. It was a very long walk, especially on cold and rainy days. But that never stopped our brother. On the way down, after selling the oranges, he would ride Kapsoula and come home. It was still a long ride downhill, but certainly more agreeable than the uphill walk.

There could have been wild animals, thieves, or enemies of my father who fought on the Communist side of the Civil War and wanted revenge. Also, in that era, ghost stories were prevalent, and for a young boy of eleven or twelve to be bold and not allow these stories to get to him is impressive; especially since in that era, ghosts stories were abundant and generally regarded as true. Not surprising, Tony had a lot of backbone and fortitude.

When it was time to go to high school—in Greece, the first six grades are grammar school; the next six are at the *gymnasio* (high school)—to be allowed to attend high school, it was required that he have a pencil, notebook, and the first year's books. As the funds for books were not an option in those trying times, Andoni asked the principal if he could borrow them, as his family had no money to purchase the books.

This principal, in his infinite stupidity and callousness, with anything but compassion or sympathy, responded by deriding and castigating my brother. He advised Andoni, in an icy, cold, demeaning manner, that "A village boy should know his place is only as a field hand." He finished his belittlement by telling him to "go back to your shack and do not waste time trying to be someone that you were never meant to be!"

Not giving up on his dream to get an education, Andoni then sent a letter to our wealthy uncle in Panama, our mother's brother, Vasilios Kourouklis. He advised our uncle of his predicament and asked if he could send ten or fifteen dollars to allow him to buy the required books. My uncle never replied. Perhaps he did not receive the letter; however, his behavior toward his sister and her family when he visited Greece in the mid-1940s suggested otherwise.

Many poor kids, destitute by the difficult life they lived, surrendered to their surroundings. But this imbecile of a principal never succeeded in making my brother feel marginal or irrelevant. As his life story clearly indicates, he never gave up. Just the opposite. I can only imagine to what heights Andoni would have reached if he had a formal education to go along with his life experience. Based on what he accomplished, his logical thought process, how he carried himself, and excellent communication skills, probably very, very far. I can only imagine the number of scars Tony suffered in his young life. But more significant, the fortitude it gave him to be the man who he eventually became—wealthy, many friends, highly respected, with a beautiful family.

All the scorn and humiliation young Andoni suffered in the village prepared him to be tougher and a better man. I imagine it was like boot camp for life's unfortunates. If you survive, you become better, tougher, and better prepared to survive and prosper. To put "icing on the cake," when he lived the American dream and became financially independent, he went back and built a beautiful, large, opulent home, embellished with marble and full of elegance. More telling, the home was built on the same plot of land where we all slept in the shack on a dirt floor.

When we came to America, Tony became the youngest president of the Kefalonian Society in the Chicagoland area at the age of twenty-two. This with only a sixth-grade education. I first learned this from Mr. Politis, the principal of Socrates Grammar School. I was given a letter for Anthony who, unbeknown to me, was its president!

Tony, in our later years, advised that there was a vote taken; he and another person with the last name of Mooeekis were nominated. Anthony was the youngest and the probably the newest member and still won the presidency. At that time he was no more than three years in America! *That* was my brother Andoni, whose peers were few, had many quality friends, loved and respected by those who knew him, and whom his brother Lou was so proud of.

Kostadina (Dina)

I considered Dina to be a person who all of us should aspire to be like. She had a clear mind, kind soul, and equanimity. The good Lord gave me many blessings; equanimity is not one of them. From what I have gathered from Kathy and Ted, Dina was a marvelous older sister. She loved all and was kind to all, and at least in my dealings she never spoke ill of anyone without good reason. Her comments were always measured.

Dina never complained to me, even though I held a grudge against her son-in-law Nick Kalouris for a very long period of time, probably well over ten years. When the rest of her family, in retribution, would boycott my events, such as my daughter's wedding or house gatherings, she would always show up, despite being beat up by age, severe arthritis in both knees, and diabetes. How can you not venerate and love such a kind and understanding soul?

Much as Nick tried to make peace in the beginning, I refused his advances, and I held on to this grudge, as noted, for well over ten years. It was my opinion that a move he made involving property, with Denny's acquiescence and assistance, disrespected my father's and my children's name. My siblings kept telling me to move on, but I could not. I always said you can hurt me and disrespect me all you want, and I will probably forgive you. But disrespecting or injuring those who I loved in any way that was not justified is a different matter. I considered Nick's actions the latter.

In hindsight, I was probably wrong in being so egotistical, and the facts at this point are nebulous and do not matter. But for Dina's sake, after ten-plus years, I did not want my sister to pass from this world without knowing that I made up with her son-in-law. I did, and I am a better person for that.

Dina had a very supportive family who truly loved her. All showed extraordinary and unconditional love as she was dying due to stage four kidney failure. It was not a pretty or serene ending. Although she will always be missed, we thank the Lord for taking her out of her immense misery.

Per Ted, Dina pretty much raised him. She was the oldest daughter, about six years older than Ted. On a nightly basis, before going to sleep, Dina would read Ted a bedtime story. She was sympathetic, loving, and an excellent role model for her younger siblings. Because I was very young when she married, I recall nothing of Dina prior to her marriage to Erotokritos (Toto).

When Dina and family came to the States, they rented a house far enough away, so we did not mingle a lot until the late stages of our lives. I was about sixteen when she arrived in America and had my own life and growing up to do. Still, the more time I spent with Dina, the more I liked her.

Dina and Toto lost a daughter, Emilia, who at the time of her death was in her early thirties. Emily was a five-seven blonde, beautiful, very kind, and very sweet. Emily married Jory Incisi and had a daughter, Christina. Emily passed from a rare form of cancer that was not treatable in that era. She continues to be missed. When Emily passed, despite their progressed age, Dina and Toto took custody of Christina, about seven years of age, and raised her.

Jory Incisi, surprisingly, did not provide any financial support for the upbringing of his daughter. Although help would have been proper and welcome, Dina and Toto never asked for any assistance. To my knowledge, Jory never offered. Their daughter's memory gave them strength and a purpose for living. Jory was not a bad a guy. I always considered him decent and still do. Perhaps when he lost Emily, he lost an important part of himself and became a bit unusual and confused. I have not seen or spoken to Jory for many years.

Christina grew up to be a beautiful and substantive person. She loves and appreciates her grandparent's dedication to her. She became a schoolteacher, married, and her firstborn was given two names: Kostandinos/Erotocritos, in honor of her grandparents. Her second son's name is Angelo. Her mother from above must be glowing with pride and happiness.

Dionisios (Denny)

As previously noted, Danny was the oldest son, smart, very generous, and well liked. During the late 1940s and early 1950s, when Greece was politically, socially, and economically in dire straits, he worked hard and was a significant contributor to the family's survival. First, he worked in construction and then for the local baker. In those days, owning a small bakery was a very big deal—so was a job in a successful bakery. If nothing else, one can provide a decent amount of bread for the family. And Denny did that and more.

I'm not certain how long Denny worked in construction. But as a side note, the contractor had a beautiful daughter about the same age or a bit younger than Danny. Her name was Olga. There is a group picture of this handsome young man in his early twenties with his arm around this beautiful young lady with blackish shoulder-length hair and elongated curls. All seemed comfortable. That picture includes me and my sister Kathy sitting on the grass and all the adults standing (our father had already left for America). The photograph suggests a good life in the village. This telling photograph is included in the appendix.

Soon after that picture was taken, Denny left Kefalonia and went and labored in the merchant marines (MM). In that era, it was typical or expected of islanders with little means and seeking their fortune to join the MM segment of the Greek economy. It is my understanding that he worked as a second cook. From personal experience, because of the cooking skills obtained in the MMs, I can categorically state it made Denny a gifted cook. At some point, at an American port, Denny jumped ship and found our father, who had already immigrated to America and made his home in Chicago.

When we arrived in Chicago, we found Danny married to a very nice and gentle person, Rosa. She was about ten years older but did not look it. Rosa was beautiful, kind, patient, and more. He and his wife just had their first child and named her Arsinoe, in honor of our mother. It is traditional for the couple to name their kids after their parents, grandparents, etc. Arsinoe was cute and a quiet baby. She grew up to be a quality mother and the foundation of her family. She married Spiro Sotiras and moved to Greece soon after. Spiro is a good, humble soul and was an acquaintance of Denny. Like my brother, he came to America illegally. Marrying Arsinoe made him legal. They have three sons and one daughter.

Spiro inherited from his father a prime coastline property in Athera, where he was born and grew up. This village is about one mile uphill from its beautiful beach. Beautiful beaches are in abundance in Kefalonia and most of Greece. When we visited Kefalonia in 2018, we met Spiro and Arsinoe for dinner at Palea Plaka, a restaurant in Argostoli. They both looked great. I was most impressed and happy with the person my niece had become. She is the backbone of that family and has worked very hard. Oftentimes, in the past, Arsinoe walked many miles, daily, to and from work. But at the end of the day, those trials and tribulations were character and foundation building. It made her smarter, stronger, and a better matriarch. Her father and mother, as I am, would be very proud of the person she has become.

Danny had many good qualities—kind, loving father, brother, and a caring friend, generous to a fault, and more. He also had shortcomings that proved disastrous. One of them was gambling. He just could not stop playing cards and often could not stop losing. Denny's and Rosie's second child was a wonderful young boy, Peter. Peter was named after his paternal grandfather. Unfortunately, our much-loved and promising young man contracted leukemia at the age of seven. At that time, this virulent disease was untreatable. Peter passed at the age of eight. I do not think any of us, and certainly not Denny and his immediate family, ever truly recovered from that huge and unexpected loss. Peter was not only too young to die but he was also Denny's most promising and caring child. He was probably the only one who Denny would listen to and the only one who could keep him on a straight and narrow path, especially if the good Lord allowed him to grow to maturity.

Case in point, when Denny should have been going home to be with his wife and seven children and to bring them food, milk, and other family needs, he was staying late at coffee shops playing cards. This young man, mature beyond his years, would call his father, pleading with him to come home. I can hear his voice even now. "*Patera, se parakalo ella spiti, se thelo* (Father, please come home. I miss you)." And my recollections suggest Denny would always heed his reasonable and mature requests.

Our Peter's sad fate still hurts. I cannot even fathom the pain and loss to my brother, Rosie, and to his siblings. All children are irreplaceable; Peter was that and more. If Peter had lived, I think my brother might have stood a chance to be a happier and a better father and husband. May my nephew rest in peace, and may there be another plane of existence so we can meet again. I believe his favorite comic hero was Batman.

Denny worked hard to feed his family. With his brains, if he channeled his strong work ethic constructively, he could have been special, probably managing the company he worked for many years, National Baking Company. Unfortunately, he did not. There is a word for that kind of personality, *asotos*. It loosely means out of control, no boundaries. Still, as previously noted, he was a caring and loving brother, father, and son. He would do anything for those he cared for. I wish he had a similar selflessness for himself.

Finally, Denny loved our mother very much, and she equally as much. The loss of his father at a very young age probably endeared him to her with a strong parental bond and he to her. Case in point, when my father passed in Kefalonia of a heart attack, Denny took responsibility for our mother and brought her to live at his house. By then, our mother was essentially blind, had bowel difficulties, and could be stubborn and sometimes hard to deal with. One fateful night, our mother was trying to find the bathroom. Feeling the wall and then finding a door, she opened it. Thinking it was the door to the bathroom, she stepped forward and tumbled headfirst down the stairs to the basement. She broke her neck. After a short stay at the hospital, our dear mother passed surrounded by her loving and heartbroken family.

Now that I am over seventy, I often reminisce how strong and generous she was before her demise in her elder hears. It saddens me as to how such a good and tough woman met such a harsh end. A couple of days prior to her passing, I visited our mom. All my siblings visited our mom on a regular basis, usually after work. To avoid bedsores, the doctor had her on a bed that would slowly vacillate from left to right, up and down—about four inches from each side. This movement, I believe was nonstop.

Knowing my mother, I do not think she enjoyed the nonstop sideways movement. One day when I visited, she said to me in Greek, "*Iia mou, onireftika ton paterasou. Mou eipa na eho epomony kai the me pari sindoma* (My Ilias, I dreamed of your father. He told me to be patient, and I will soon come to get you)." She appeared relieved she would be finally rid of her suffering. About a day or two later, thanks to the Almighty, he kept his word.

When our mother was taken in by Denny, I was aware he was receiving our mom's very small social security, which was originally our father's. The rest of us occasionally pitched in with a bit of financial help. In hindsight, that was nowhere near enough and a mere pittance for the responsibility, stress, and commitment he and especially Rosa experienced on a fairly regular basis. Concurrently, they had six children to raise. Peter had already passed. Without question, Rosa was a saint and a wonderful and beloved mother.

Besides his beloved Peter, Denny and Rosa were blessed to have six additional children: Arsinoe, Anastasia, Gerasimos, Kostadinos, Nickolaos, and Eva. Except for Peter, who passed from leukemia at the age of eight, all grew up to become responsible and productive adults, parents, and spouses. Denny's third son, Nick, passed in his early thirties. He was smart and competent. In fact, prior to his death, he was an excellent mechanic and had opened his own shop and gas station. In addition to gas services and maintenance, Nick also repaired vehicles. I do not recall the cause of death. Nick had a military funeral, as he served in the army. To date, in the United States, no other Garbis or Markadonatos has served in the military. I almost did, during the Vietnam era. But my lottery number was high enough, and I was attending college, so I was given a pass. For a few good reasons, which I will not articulate, as they are not relevant to this book, the Vietnam War was generally not popular with the American people. As a result, most of our returning soldiers did not receive the respect and adulation they so richly deserved.

While all of Denny's children have done well, Stacy (Anastasia), his second-oldest daughter, has proven to be a force to be reckoned with as a businesswoman and relative. Most importantly, as a wonderful wife, mother, aunt, and yes, niece. When Nick passed, Stacey and Tom, her spouse, took responsibility and raised Nick's two young daughters as if they were their own. Eventually, both married two fine young men. Their weddings and education were funded by Stacy and Tom. Without Stacy and her uncompromising tough love, I am certain that would not have been possible. There were too many obstacles for two bright and independent-minded very young ladies. Sadly, their blood mother was very nice but had an alcohol addiction that continued for a time. Nick had his own demons; they got married young and ended up getting divorced after seven years.

Eleftherios (Ted)

Ted proved to be a good and dependable son. As a young lad of no more than fifteen years of age, he worked for neighbors in the fields by Vlahata. Ted also worked in construction, digging up gravel to make cement and asbestos, and wherever else he could find work. He was a good son and contributed to the family's survival.

When Ted was very young, he would on occasion plead for more food. This is normal for a young child, too young to realize what was happening around him. And for most, hunger was the norm, not the exception. Unfortunately, this was a period of famine, and many Greeks died or suffered immensely from malnutrition and an inadequate food supply. Asking for more food on one too many occasions was too much for a tired, wasted father who worked hard but still could not provide enough to feed his family. Wrap around the stress due to the food shortage, our father also partook in World War II and the viciously bloody Greek Civil War. He also had a temper that did not surface a lot, but when it did it could be almost uncontrollable, with potentially disastrous results.

After one of those occasions of Ted relentlessly complaining for more food, but more food could not be found, our father snapped. With a thoughtless, impulsive response, full of uncontrolled anger, he grabbed young Ted by the neck and kept squeezing. Ted's eyes almost popped out of his eye sockets, until my mother and the rest of the family brought our father back to reality. I emphasize "reality" because thoughtless and blind rage appears to be a Garbis affliction; at least for some of us. I think my father, Bill, Tony, and I have (had) this affliction. Some more than others. It does not rear its ugly head often, but when it does it can be a danger for all involved—the angry one and the recipient of this anger. We, the inflicted ones, must find a way to train our minds to always be in control of this highly unpredictable and dangerous rage. Unfortunately, easier said than done.

I witnessed Tony's potential for blind rage while we were unloading a truck in the ally by Lawrence and Western in Chicago. We were moving our parents and me to an apartment on Washtenaw Street. I was in my late teens at that time. We had no choice but to block the ally to unload. Two young men in their early twenties, sitting in their car, in frustration for being forced to wait, were yelling ethnic slurs about the Greeks. After a bit, Tony got uncontrollably enraged and started screaming at them, "Better shut up! You hear me? Shut up!" And with every breath, his voice became louder and more ominous and foreboding. Concurrently, he started running as fast as he could toward their car, which by this time, seeing that crazy man chasing them, floored the car going backward to escape. Lucky for them, they did. I never witnessed Dina, Ted, or Kathy lose control and just go for it. They are the lucky ones.

Ted is a very smart and a blessed man. Sadly, in his youth, Ted had the most difficult life of all the siblings. The reason: he was left-handed. The governing thought of that period—and probably into the fifties, sixties, and beyond—was that left-handed people were either cursed and brought bad luck, or their condition caused a lower level of intelligence than right-handed people. Hence it was the mission of the right-dominant humans in Greece and most of Europe to take measures to correct this "infirmity." As a result, those born left-handed were frequently punished with the objective of converting them to right-hand dominant. Not an easy conversion, and this perception was totally erroneous and ill conceived. The customary method of conversion was by physical punishment or mental torture or both. This includes derogatory remarks and nonstop ridicule in public, implying stupidity, usually all at the same time.

As a young lad, Ted was punished by his teacher and others and to a much lesser extent by his immediate family for being left-handed. He was repeatedly laughed at and publicly humiliated. I cannot imagine the amount of physical and mental torture that this normal young man experienced because he was born left-handed. I cannot imagine what went through his mind and how insecure he must have felt. To stay grounded as he is, he must have been blessed with a strong will and strong mind.

I know I am second-guessing, as my father was a smart and loving father. He had common sense and compassion. For example, for his brother, Athanasios who had contracted Consumption (Tuberculosis), he risked all because he was intelligent enough to know how to protect his family and still be a humane person to those inflicted with TB. I wish he had been smart enough to recognize that the general perception of left-handed people was in error and stopped the family and his teacher from abusing Ted with mental and physical cruelty. I recognize I am not being fair, and yes, I admit this is my "Monday-morning quarterback" moment.

This stupidity reached its highest level when students from ten districts from various parts of Greece congregated in Kalavrita, located in Peloponnesus. As a matter of background and from a historical perspective, this town became famous with patriotic reverence after six hundred Greek rebels at the Monastery of Agia Lavra received the blessings of Bishop Germanos on March 21, 1821, to begin the fight for Greek independence. The revolutionaries then proceeded and liberated the town of Kalavrita. This after four hundred long, painful years in bondage. This was the beginning of the end of Turkish domination of Greece. As an aside, the real fustanella (Greek kilt) has four hundred pleats, each symbolizing one of the four hundred years of bondage.

At this gathering, there was a contest for all the students in attendance. I do not know the actual head count, but there must have been a sizeable number, since ten districts from all areas of Greece partook in this excursion. One hundred students would not be a bad guess. Ted supports this number and possibly higher. Each student was asked to draw the local church and the surrounding landscape. Ted won first prize! While receiving his award, the leader of this event asked Ted's teacher if he was his best student. With a trite, belittling response, this teacher responded, "No, on the contrary, he is the worst." Can you believe the imbecilic stupidity of this so-called "teacher?" Hello! Ted won first prize, you dumb shit! Young Ted heard this, and to this day, in his late seventies, he still feels the pain. I, too, feel the pain for this fine brother of mine.

Through no doing of his own, Ted was blessed to be born left-handed. Unfortunately, in that period, very few people knew it was a gift, not a curse. Ted was anything but stupid. He is witty, smart, and very funny. He and his wife, Irene, got the last laugh. They are blessed with four beautiful children—Gerasimos, Anastasia, Niki, and Antonis—and double blessed with eight wonderful grandchildren. His children all have become successful and a credit to the Garbis and Marinakos families. Anastasia (Stacy) is a partner and lead counsel in a national law firm. The rest are successful business owners. All are fine people. His wife, Irene, keeps them all grounded. She is a blessing to the Garbis clan in many positive ways.

A recent study suggests left-handed people might have certain advantages right-handed people do not possess. For example, this study identified the advantage of eloquence and perhaps creativity. Ted has both but especially one in abundance. His humor is so smooth and naturally funny. He could have made it big as a stand-up comic or in the movies as a comedian and more. His demeanor is likeable and pleasant.

Finally, my brief readings on the topic of why Europe for a long period punished left-handed people suggest that we have the ancient Greeks to thank. The ancient Greeks thought left-handed people brought bad luck. I do not know the reason this highly intelligent people, who gifted so much wisdom and education to the world, came to this unfortunate conclusion.

Another, more viable reason for this perception relates to the times of antiquity, when the phalanx formation was engaged in battle. For example, if you were left-handed, the very important protective wall of shields would have a weak spot where the left-hander was next to a right-handed soldier. This could cause weakness and possible collapse of the phalanx, which could prove disastrous.

It was unfortunate for the left-handed people of Europe, since the Romans idolized the ancient Greeks, probably spread this fiction throughout Europe with similar repercussions. Perhaps the phalanx concern eventually morphed into "bad luck" and further on to a lower level of intelligence.

Although I was not born at that time, I still feel pain for young Ted. So grateful that he was mentally strong and unyielding to not allow false perceptions of reality to take him down. I celebrate the man and person he grew to be—first-class gentleman, respected and liked by all who know him. This includes his brother Ilias. Despite his difficult childhood, he is very forgiving—unlike his brother Lou!

Kathy

My sister Kathy helped raise me. When I was young, she was essentially my caretaker. There is no doubt she loved her baby brother and was kind and caring. Perhaps this is why we are still very close. When I was born, she was probably about seven years of age. As previously noted, in the appendix, there is a picture of the family and friends, all standing, except a few. The few included me and Kathy sitting on the grass. I must have been five, and she twelve. It is uncanny how my son George and daughter Katherine looked so much like me and Kathy when they were of similar age. As we got older, that comparison was no longer reasonable. For George, the better. Katerina held her own and then some. But her competition was my sister Kathy, who, unlike her brother Louis, grew up to be a rare and natural beauty, wrapped around family values, kindness, and more.

As with Dina, I do not know much of Kathy's young life when we lived in Greece. Because of her kind, loving demeanor and rare beauty, and despite being only sixteen or possibly seventeen, she had several suitors when she arrived in America, all in their late twenties or early thirties. This included at least one teacher named Karnezis. Also, I believe one person from our village—from the family of Minetos and about Tony's age—came as far as New York with the hopes of marrying Kathy. He returned to Kefalonia when he found out his wish was not possible, as she was recently engaged. Kathy never knew he had feelings for her.

Kathy became engaged and married George Phillipopoulos. He was twenty-eight years old, handsome and about five seven. He was a good person, measured, thoughtful, considerate and religious. Most importantly, he was an excellent provider and a dedicated husband and father. My recollection is that he saw and fell in love with Kathy in her brief stint in the church choir. It may also have been in a dance hall, probably sponsored by the church so that young Greek folks can mingle and become better acquainted and perhaps, find their match. Irrespective of which or both, George and Kathy found their match. Together they raised five children—Peter, John, Helen, Renna and Gerasimos, in that order. Finally, being married that young was not rare in those days, especially for old-school thinking from the village.

My memories of George are all pleasant and remind me of the quality person who he was. Sadly, and unexpectedly, George was killed in an occupational accident at work on January 5, 1977. A disastrous loss for his family, comprised of a young wife (about thirty-three years old) with five young children, the oldest being roughly thirteen years of age and the youngest about four. George's death sent a huge ripple of sadness and loss to all who knew and loved him. Furthermore, the family leadership he exuded was now broken. I remember that all our family was flown to LA and back home, including my brother-in-law Erotocritos and my cousin Nick Kourouklis. All transportation was paid by George's employer, United Airlines. Key management came to George's home, more than once. They were respective, accommodating and expressed sympathy with class.

I rarely cried as a young man and held it together. Much as I tried, not this time. Seeing my poor sister feeling lost and helpless, and because of hers and the children's disastrous and tragic loss, my heart could not take it anymore. I went outside as quietly as I could, and solitarily began to cry. My poor father figured out what was happening, came outside and with tearful eyes, patted me in the back and tried to speak but could not. The prevalent unimaginable and extreme pain experienced by our family choked and rendered him speechless. Still, I clearly understood him. He wanted to tell me how proud he was of me. Although I, too, loved my father, I was too young to express those exact similar feelings. In my old age, I think of him fondly and I now realize the sacrifices, love and commitment he gave to his family and I say, "Father, I think of you daily, and now it is my turn to get moist tears and symbolically and surreally give you a pat on the back and thank you for all that you sacrificed and did for family and country!"

The person who recommended the law firm that was retained was a policeman who also happened to be a neighbor and friend. I have forgotten his name. I recall he was also going to law school, and as the results suggest, provided good counsel.

In the beginning, I assisted Bill and Tony in interviewing perspective lawyers, but I had to return to work back in Chicago. Bill and Tony did a wonderful job in finalizing the details. This resulted in a very good financial settlement for Kathy and the children. I assume the third-party settlement was totally paid by the firm that owned the food truck and employed the driver involved in the accident. I also assume it was an independent contractor to United Airlines.

The workers' compensation benefits were statutory and automatic to the widow and children. These additional funds were very helpful to Kathy and descendants in helping them find any semblance of normalcy, if one could be found. I may be wrong, but the children received the monthly benefits until at least the age of eighteen and possibly more if they went to school; Kathy received them until she was remarried. Thankfully, George's memory was embedded firmly in the children's minds. All grew up to be industrious, excellent, and caring parents.

When we went to George's wake, we got in line to pay our respects to our dear and departed brother-in-law. When my turn came, and saw him in the casket, it was obvious that the severity of the injury was the cause of his death. When I bent down to pay my respects, seeing George as he was transformed by the injuries, I became uncomfortable and sad. Tony, who was right behind me, saw that mentally I was a starting to lose it. Seeing this, he grabbed me by my shoulders and quickly got me back to normalcy, and I moved on, as there was a line of people behind us, waiting to pay their respects.

Some of the memories as a nine-or-so-year-old involving George include:

- He introduced me to avocados. At first the taste was not agreeable. In time, I began to enjoy this "fruit," which also has health benefits—most notably, cardiovascular.
- When George first kissed Kathy, I believe it was in our dining room when we lived at Van Buren and Cicero, Chicago, Illinois. I happened to be nearby. George, respective and apprehensive, said, "Please don't tell your parents." I kiddingly said, "Give me a quarter, and I won't." And I believe he did.
- When he worked on the weekends, George would take Bill and me with him to the factory that employed him. I assume this was catch-up work or overtime. The factory was empty. He allowed us to check out the large warehouse. We noted countless bags filled with product, stacked to about seven to ten feet in height. I do not recall their contents, but it appeared to be granular. The fun began when we discovered that this vacant warehouse had forklifts. On one of those occasions, when we drove and raced, I crashed into a section of the stacked bags, and the one near the top was split open, and the contents were dripping profusely to the floor. We both stopped, left the lift trucks where I crashed, and went to find George. We never spoke to George of my "accident," just played dumb!
- George was a big hockey fan. He took me at least once to a Blackhawks hockey game. Because of the significant violence allowed in games at that time, which generally ended up having broken nose and blood on the rink, I never became a big fan of this sport. Baseball, football, and basketball, in that order, are the games I enjoy watching—if we win!
- In my teens (mid-1960s), I flew to California when school was out, probably for the summer, and spent a week or two at their house that they had recently purchased at 128 S. Prospect Ave, Redondo Beach. They were very kind and generous. They even took me to see for the first time the original Disney World Park. It was a wondrous and unforgettable experience. They never accepted any money from me. So, to show my appreciation for their kind and generous ways, before departing for Chicago, I purchased a little something for the house.
- The one memory deeply embedded in my mind are his comments to me when he, in a small pickup truck, company owned, took me

with to keep him company. It was probably a weekend and most likely a Saturday. On the way back, as he was driving, a young boy on his tricycle drove into the street by mistake. This was a main road, probably Central Avenue, Chicago. Near the child on the tricycle was a huge city lamp post.

I am certain we were not speeding, but it was still too fast to "stop on a dime." When George saw the child and its proximity to us, he turned the wheel toward the lamppost, braked immediately and hard, causing us to skid. Thankfully, we stopped before hitting the lamppost and avoided injuring the child. He then made a very revealing and memorable statement: "Ilia mou, better we get hit and die than the child." This speaks volumes of the compassion and humanity of my late brother-in-law George.

After a few years passed, Kathy met and married John Givens, a good and likeable person. John was employed as a manager in the ticket agent section of United Airlines. He knew George, as they both worked for the UAL, Los Angeles. He was also a Vietnam veteran. I am certain he tried to work with George's descendants and be a good stepfather. At best, empirical evidence suggest his efforts produced mixed results. And that is understandable. In the eyes of the very young and strong-willed children, he could never replace George. From their marriage, Kathy and John had two daughters. Sadly, John passed due to cancer on June 23, 2011, at the relatively young age of sixty-four.

Finally, George's five descendants grew up to be measured and successful in business and as parents. Their grandkids are beautiful and smart. Much of the beauty must come from Kathy, and much of the business acumen from George—and perhaps in regard to drive, with an effective touch from the Garbis side. George, may your memory be eternal, and may it continue to bless your Kathy and your descendants!

Vasilios (Bill) of Greece

My brother Bill was a very handsome young man when he reached adulthood. In the section that follows, I will share with you a few of my reasons why I consider Bill so special and the best from all the siblings, including yours truly. In this section, I will share what little I know of his early childhood in Vlahata. There is an incident or two in his youth that you may find funny and a precursor of what one could expect from Bill as an adult.

Bill was what you would call in Greek *zoiros*, difficult to control. This loosely translates to "a child who is headstrong and unruly," not rebellious, but he did what he did because he thought it right, or it was fun. He was willing to take risks if the objective was justified. A prime example that comes to mind involves a neighbor who was also a friend of my father's, Mr. Bosovikos. I do not recall his firsts name. Bill could not have been more than seven or eight years old when he found Bosovikos sitting on a bench holding his head in his hands, eyes closed, and contemplating his sad state in life. No job or resources to provide for his family. Bosovikos was one of the many with this fundamental concern. He was thinking to himself, "Lord, where will the next meal come from? How will I feed my children?" Those were hard times in Kefalonia and most of Greece. World War II had ended, and without any respite, the brutal civil war commenced and had just recently ended.

As Bosovikos sat on a bench pondering his fate, he felt a very hard, swift slap in his face, opposite of the side where his head was resting in his hand. His eyes opened just in time to see this young boy running as fast as the wind to escape. Like a wounded bull that thirsted for revenge, Bosovikos started chasing Bill, and at the same time swearing, cursing, and threatening him as to how he would skewer him, calling Bill every derogatory name he could muster! Much as he tried, thankfully for Bill, he could not catch him. Like his father before him, Bill was just too fast. Bosovikos later laughingly shared with his friend, my father, "Lucky for Bill that he was not caught. In my rage, I would have killed him!"

Bill was not punished for this behavior. Probably because, in his way of thinking, he had a good reason for this action. Apparently, prior the aggressive slap attack, Bosovikos seemed to have had an argument in which he appeared to physically threaten our father. Bill heard or witnessed this verbal diatribe and took exception. Being protective of family, he determined that it was time for payback for this unneighborly neighbor. Mr. Bosovikos did not retaliate and laughed at Bill's bold action. He probably understood and admired this gutsy boy for having the backbone to defend his father. As he grew to maturity, Bill had a proclivity to always find ways to take care of his family. That is why I consider Bill the best of us! Without exception, he cared for all.

Harassing Bosovikos did not end there. Soon after the slap, Mr. Bosovikos was tending his small plot of land that was by the shoreline near Trapezaki. This is a very well-known landmark about a half mile downhill from where we lived, very close to the shore. It is a natural phenomenon that is shaped in the form of a table that rises about thirty feet near the water's edge. *Trapezaki* means "little table" in Greek. Bill, from a high ground and far enough away, started throwing rocks at him. Finally, Bosovikos had enough. He visited our mom and told her that she better get a hold of her son, or else. After that, Bill, behaved and stopped harassing Mr. Bosovikos. Apparently, he decided that he had dished out enough punishment so that Bosovikos would no longer threaten our father.

Finally, when Bill was a boy of four or five, he was either climbing up the side of our house, which was about two stories high, or he was horsing around and fell from the balcony. Irrespective, he slipped and fell to the ground, and his head hit hard on a rock. Bill could not be awakened. My poor father, seeing his lifeless body, was devasted. He picked up Bill, and with total resignation he tossed his lifeless body onto the bed, thinking his son was dead. As soon as the body hit the bed, blood began gushing out of the back of Bill's head and miraculously, my brother was alive and well! Thank you, Lord! It would be hard to imagine life without Bill. I am confident our father loved all but probably Bill a bit more as he saw a lot of himself in Bill. I believe all his children would agree with this statement, especially yours truly.

If Bill had died, it would have been a huge loss to the family. For one, when Bill grew up and had his own business in America, he was a heck of a brother to all of us. We played fast ball pitching by a school yard by his house and became best friends in our older years. He was a smart, resourceful and a successful businessman. With his spouse, Susan, they raised two children: a beautiful daughter, Arsinoe (Noula), and a handsome son, Alex; both successful and competent adults, parents, and spouses. Everybody loved Bill. He was witty, funny, and always had his family's back. He even learned and flew a one-propeller airplane! Indeed, Bill was selfless and an all-around good brother and relative.

Bill of America

As previously mentioned under the "Siblings" section, the cause of Bill's death was a ruptured heart artery. By the time he was taken by ambulance to the hospital, he had passed. I believe I felt the time of his death. Prior to passing, I received a call from Susan, his spouse, advising that he had a heart attack and was taken to the hospital. Susan is a wonderful relative and was a very supportive spouse and mother. I was with Phyllis on the highway speeding as fast as I could toward the hospital when I felt something briefly passing through my heart. At that moment I solemnly told Phyllis that my brother just died. I would have given anything to have been proven wrong …

Bill was so, so, *so* special in so many positive ways. He was kind, considerate, loved his family, relatives, and had many quality and loyal friends. Many of his friends loved him and called him "brother." Bill was funny and thoughtful. He was the best of relatives, and prior to his death we became close friends. I can only share some of the things he did for me:

- I had allergic reaction in the mid-1990s. After taking a drug called Seldane to minimize allergic reactions, I would get hyper around midnight and have bad feelings. The bad feelings would manifest as an inclination to do harm to my family—so unlike me, but true. I called Bill twice when I had these ominous feelings. He was the one person who I loved and trusted enough to help me through this uncomfortable and dangerous predicament. Twice he came during the midnight hours, calmed me down, and then I would go to sleep. Another side effect of this drug was a feeling of emptiness and lifeless with NO energy or drive. When I advised Bill of my symptoms, he took me to a doctor at a Loyola Medical Center for some tests. The doctor examined me and found nothing wrong. He then asked if I was happy with my family and were there any reason to be depressed. I said, "No, on the contrary, I have a great family, wife, kids, and work is great." On the way back from the examination, right past Seventy-Fifth on Naper and Plainfield Road, I abruptly asked Bill to immediately stop the car. I got out and promptly threw up. As I threw up, it felt like life and energy were oozing back into me, and I was normal again. I never had that feeling before or after. I was surprised that that drug was still in my system for at least five days

after ingesting it. I later found out that Seldane was discontinued soon after due to several suicides that were attributed to this drug.
- In 1992, when I decided to leave Corroon and Black and start my own brokerage firm, I asked Bill if he could lend me $5,000. My reasoning was that if C & B fought the departure, as the annual revenues I produced for my employer were significant, it could be a prolonged and an expensive legal battle. I needed to have enough funds to support my family for a month or two. By then revenues would flow in from the companies that followed me in my departure.

Key companies were Tang (largest minority owned company in the United States in the 1990s), OSI Industries (McDonald's largest supplier of meat worldwide), and MTH (medium-size company), with a fantastic name and reputation, in the glazing and iron works world. MTH was renowned nationally, for the superior worked product they provided. In fact, MTH won first prize nationally in its industry for the work performed for the O'Hara terminal. After a few years passed, MTH also constructed the Cloud Gate (the Bean) and many more edifices that were primarily located in Chicago. The Cloud Gate appears to be MTH's crowning glory. When Chicago is advertised or shown worldwide, this one of the monuments always included.

I also had a concern that if my soon-to-be ex-employer sued, he may ask and be granted an estoppel of revenues to be received until the case was resolved. And the estoppel could last for a long period of time resulting in significant costs and burden to me. If this happened and I already had received a good amount of the funds, my thinking was that I *may* be able to outlast the litigation.

Thankfully, John Sullivan was the president of C and B, and we settled out of court for a very modest settlement. Due to local law, it could have been twice the value of my portfolio, which was substantial and rapidly growing, primarily due to significant international growth by OSI. I did have a noncompete. Fortunately, in that era, enforceability of an employment contract was not an automatic. Most significant, John Sullivan, the president of C and B and a friend, was a class act. One small example of John's class is that after settling and severing all business ties with C and B, I had difficulty approaching a needed insurer. Because of size and newness of my firm, John helped me get to that insurer. I have not seen John for many years. Nevertheless, I will never forget his magnanimity and class. The same goes for Guy Sisto (Tang Industries) and Vytas Ambutas (Tang Industries), Dan Ljubenko and Scot Schwarting of (OSI Industries), and Lyle Hill (MTH). From the insurer side, Bryan Hollowell of Saint Paul Travelers, Mark Willis, president of AIG North America and Timothy Szerlong, SVP, Chubb Chicago.

In the incipient stage of my company, these were the key insurers for the type of business I serviced. The most important and supportive were Mark Willis by far, then Tim Szerlong. Many more underwriters came forth after the acceptance by the aforementioned. To them, too, I owe much. After a while, I had access to most insurers except those that had specialty programs that preferred a specialty broker. It was essential that the key insurers that serviced or could service these large and complex accounts were willing to work with a one-man shop.

Despite a potential huge risk (broker misappropriations in that era were not uncommon) and despite the pressures imposed on them by my ex-employer, they decided in my favor. I had interfaced with these insurers on a regular and mutually beneficial basis for a few years. They knew my work ethic and my abilities as marketing manager, producer, and account executive. They saw me as a no-nonsense, honorable, and effective broker whose word was his law; and I tried to be that and more. They deserved it, my ancestors deserved it and my family deserved it! No amount of money is worth a tarnished name and reputation. Honor and respect was always integrated in our work ethic; also, never cut corners, appreciated the huge fiduciary responsibilities they have bestowed upon us, and strive for excellence were some of the other attributes we aspired to adhere to.

These and more constituted our preamble and commitment to our clients and underwriters. And we followed it religiously. For the sake of full disclosure, having such quality global organizations as clients was a significant factor in an underwriters' decision to work with me. Because of their commitment and support, I reciprocated by providing our valued clients with the best service and support I and my employees could offer. Cost or time was never an issue, and I knew they would try to find ways to reciprocate. And they did with their trust, friendship, business, and understanding.

It was an honest and sincere partnership that benefitted all. The principal focus was always on the clients. In time, because of our commitment to quality, excellence, and honesty, strong friendships developed that will last a lifetime. As I settled with C and B reasonably quickly, I paid Bill the loan the following month, with much appreciation for his support.

- Because I had a very demanding and successful business that was quickly growing on a global scale, especially in the mid-1990s, I was very stressed. As a result, Bill decided that he and I should go to Greece for a vacation and booked a trip in business class on United Airlines. At that time, Bill and Tony were not close. There was an argument between Bill and Tony's wife (Antoinette) that Tony took exception to. After we departed from O'Hare, I was trying to find ways to make peace between the two. Every time Bill thought and spoke about Tony, his voice would get louder and louder.

For those that do not travel to Europe, it is usually an evening flight and after an hour or two, people with windows lower the shades and try to sleep. I noticed that the traveler right in front of us, to my right, was twitching and moving in a troubling, irritated way, expressing displeasure that this matter was discussed so loudly. I happen to look at the back of his head and neck and that silhouette reminded me of someone that if I were correct, could jeopardize a key client-OSI Industries. I quietly asked Bill to please keep it down if he valued my business welfare.

After Bill settled a bit, just so I can get a better look at the justifiably irritated person in front of us, I got up to go to the bathroom. On my way back to my seat, this gentleman got up. I said "Bill! How nice to see you!" He replied, "Hi, Lou," and went to the bathroom. Thereafter we were as quiet as a cemetery. That irritated person was Bill Weimer, senior VP and CFO of OSI Industries. By far my largest and most lucrative client. OSI, USA, provided on a worldwide basis, all the beef, bacon, and chicken to McDonald's and its myriad of locations. We knew each other well due to our meetings at OSI's corporate office in Aurora and because OSI had recently purchased the largest chicken processing factory in Europe-Moy Park (MP). As result, we also interfaced a couple of times in Ireland. At that time (mid-1990s), MP processed roughly 37 percent of all chickens sold in Europe. Soon thereafter, OSI also purchased Padley's located in England. Padley's was also one of the larger chicken processing facilities in Europe but not quite the size of Moy Park. Combined, they had at least twelve thousand employees and exceeded if my memory is correct, roughly a billion plus in sales. When we landed, my client and I exchanged goodbyes and well-wishes.

When I returned from my vacation in Kefalonia, I went to visit with the risk manager of OSI, Scot Schwarting. Laughing, Scot shared that Bill Weimer requested to always let him know when and where Garbis was traveling overseas. This way, Bill advised, he can make certain to take a different flight! It was, of course, in gest. Weimer was a good man and good to me. That is also true for all the OSI Leadership that I engaged, until there was a change in a key management position (treasury).

The previous Treasurer, George Krasinski unexpectedly died of cancer and was replaced. After sixteen mutually beneficial and highly productive years, the replacement of a quality deceased professional, who also developed into a good friend, resulted in my losing the total account.

The new Treasurer awarded this very valuable and visible account to AON, second-largest property and casualty insurance broker in the world. AON had tried for over twelve years to undermine and replace me without success. They just could not be competitive and probably, their day-to-day services did not match our quality and effectiveness.

OSI had a very demanding and professional risk manager, Scot Schwarting. He was well liked, smart and respected by all that interfaced with him. Our mutual commitment to excellence made us better professionals, and motivated each other to do the best we can for the OSI Group and we did. In time, we also became and to this day, are good friends. Together we made a significant financial and asset protection difference to OSI. Unfortunately, for personal reasons, he left OSI.

With Mr. Krasinski's passing, and the concurrent departure of Scot, the new treasurer had an easy path for replacing us. As result, after fifteen-plus years of a symbiotic and mutually beneficial partnership, Aon was awarded this lucrative account. It is my understanding that AON was the firm that introduced the new treasurer to OSI.

Irrespective, such changes in brokers are not rare. This is part of the cost of doing business in a very competitive and desirable field. At the end of the day, I will always have fine memories of that special time in my life where not only it was financially impactful, but most important, we, as a team (client and broker), made a significant difference to OSI's risk management and its bottom line. And while doing so, we became better and smarter brokers in our chosen field. There is plenty of documentation to support this observation.

- When I purchased the North Aurora office building, I renamed it Garbis Properties in honor of my father, who had recently passed. Bill brought me as a gift, a huge mural depicting various Hellenic arts and crafts of antiquity, including topless women, a harp, vases, and more. Its intent was to make a statement on the significant extent of the growth in arts and science by the ancient Greeks. The mural is roughly two feet vertical in height and six feet horizontally. The three-dimensional mural appears to have been shaped using molded plaster with the characters and objects protruding out of the mural.
- Because I was getting obese (close to three hundred pounds) due to stress and accompanying apnea, he bought me a treadmill that was huge and expensive. I never asked him to. It was a surprise, but Bill cared for his brother despite my bad habits and wanted to try his best to help me stay healthy.
- At my previous house in Wheeling, my bathroom floor was not in good shape. Bill decided to stop by one day and fix me a new floor. It took him quite a bit of time and effort. And yet there he was. Admittedly it was not the best construction as it was probably his first time putting down a floor but that did not matter. It was an improvement. Most importantly, it was my brother, Bill, working hard and taking valuable time from his work and family to improve his brother's place.
- He bought my son George a huge tricycle when he was two years old. That was not a cheap gift. It may have had a battery-powered engine. Bill liked all my kids but probably George a bit more, since he was called George William. George for Phyllis's father and William for her mother. I, expanded for self-serving reasons to include my late brother-in-law George Phillipopoulos and my brother Bill (William).
- Bill took lessons and learned how to fly a single propeller airplane. After showing me how he performed a thorough checklist of items required prior to flight, he took me up for about a half-hour ride, right over the Southside of Chicago. I am certain I was not the only person Bill showed kindness and generosity to. As previously noted, he had many good friends who treated him like a brother. It is not surprising.

When Bill died, Peter Masters, a longtime friend of Bill's that was and is an accomplished and published Greek poet, wrote a wonderful and touching poem that was put to Greek Music. I remember that the key storyline was that all his friends were at their regular gathering place (coffee shop), at the usual agreed time. Waiting and waiting and waiting and waiting, until they received a message that Bill had died.

Bill's passing was a totally shock to all. He was in shape and looked healthy. Among all of us, he was the most beloved for many good reasons, a few cited above. He is still missed and often spoken about in a nostalgic, mournful way. But then again, we remind ourselves that life is not a guarantee, and our cup is always half full, never half empty. We were blessed to have had our beloved brother for fifty-five years. How many families lose loved ones, much earlier? How many families will have family members who will never be whole? How many families have seen loved ones die of starvation? Bottom Line, life is a gift, and we must be thankful for whatever amount blessings and time we have or had with our loved ones on this earth.

CHAPTER 3

Childhood Memories

The comments and observations that follow are things I remember or was told. My parents and older siblings where the primary source of confirmation or adding to my recollections as a very young lad in Kefalonia. In regard to historical events, I researched history books and articles. If I have improperly slandered or misrepresented anyone or anything, my apologies. It was unintentional. If I state negative comments on individuals, be assured I have found them to be accurate. Irrespective of who the individual discussed is, we need to maintain honesty on contents and not base it on fiction.

I have verified most of my recollections. If I must guess, at least 95 percent has been confirmed. To my surprise, based on confirmation from my siblings, much of my recollections were spot on. Still, changes and refinements had to be made after speaking with Tony, Ted, and Kathy. All three verified, clarified, and expanded my childhood memories, especially Tony. Till the end, his memory was as sharp as ever. Tony and I have several traits in common. Unfortunately, a sharp memory is not one of them.

Until the age of thirty or so, memories of my youth were dormant. Then it was as if the floodgates opened, and my mind was inundated with many memories of this young boy's life in the village. Although it sounds outlandish to be true, the Zografia memory that is discussed in the pages that follow was confirmed by Tony, Ted, and Kathy.

My earliest memory is of my second-oldest brother, Antoni (Tony). I recall being carried on his shoulders and waddling in the shallows of our white, sandy beach, Trapezaki. I was two years old at that time. It seems surreal, but even now I can see this little boy with fat cheeks on his big brother's shoulders, gazing down in a sleepy, lazy trance in amazement at the diamond shapes that the sun's rays reflected on the glistening water. Coincidentally, a large fish lazily swam not too far from us. Tony must have been a wonderful big brother. My memory of him suggests to me that I felt very safe on his shoulders. I am told that when any of the family would discipline or punish me, I would cry out "Antoni mou (my Anthony)!" pleading for him to save me from punishment.

My second and most vivid memory is of the August 12, 1953, earthquake. It was roughly three months short of my third birthday. The earthquake devasted much of Kefalonia and the nearby island of Zakynthos. One side of the island (southwest side), in the capital city, Argostoli, small waterfront sections partly sank into the sea. On the southeastern part, it rose by approximately sixty centimeters, roughly two feet. I assume the measurements included a visual of the watermarks prior to and after the earthquake.

The earthquake struck at about 11:23 a.m. local time. Between six hundred and one thousand people were killed, and roughly ten thousand were left homeless, with one thousand injured. The epicenter appears to have been near Argostoli (capital city of Kefalonia) and Lixouri (second-largest city and about a mile or two across the water from Argostoli). Britain, Sweden, and Norway provided aid. It appears the English were the first responders and most generous. Even three Israeli military vessels that were nearby heard the stress call and came to assist. Not surprising that England was most generous, since Kefalonia was one of the Greek islands they controlled until roughly 1860.

Tony, who was fourteen years of age at that time, advised that before the earthquake began the gulf by Vlahata changed to a blackish color from the normal sky-blue clear waters that it was before and after. Then suddenly all hell broke loose; the earth started to violently tremble. I'm not certain how long the tremors lasted, but it was enough to make our home uninhabitable. Tony also mentioned that after the earthquake stopped, he saw an old man aimlessly walking in the street as if he had surrendered his will to live. He must have lost all that mattered to him—his loved ones. A sad story, but not unique.

I am guessing our home was built with wood, stucco, and masonry. I remember my mother jumping on top of me and covering me with her body to avoid debris from the seemingly collapsing home. Luckily, the main part of the home that we slept in did not collapse; however, because it was too dangerous to inhabit, it was razed. There were two other smaller structures—the outhouse and the kitchen. Both were destroyed by the earthquake. The wood and other useful material partly went to Toto, Dina's husband, as part or in total of a dowry; the rest was used to build the shack where we lived in for roughly three years.

My next memory is that we lived in this small wooden shack right below where the house stood. As noted above, the material used for the shed was obtain from the razed house. I remember my mother putting a blanket on the dirt floor and a second one to cover me, heating fist-size stones and placing them on the four corners of the top blanket to keep me warm. This memory must have been in winter. This is a reasonable assumption, since the earthquake occurred in early August.

I remember a four- or five-feet-deep crevice that opened on the property that was near our house. I do not recall how far the crevice ran, but it seemed lengthy to a very young boy. Also, my memory tells me that the crevice was on farmland east of us, not on a main road.

Once the earthquake started, multiple earthquake shocks followed of different strengths. The worst measured 7.3 on the Richter scale. Seismologists advise that total destruction occurs at 8 or greater. Under the Mercalli Intensity Scale, it was rated (X) extreme; XII suggests total destruction. It can be deduced that both provided a similar conclusion. The difference is, the Mercalli Scale describes the intensity based on observable effects; the Richter scale is based on energy released by the earthquake. Finally, in 1953, at least in the island of Kefalonia, even well-built homes were not constructed to withstand significant earthquakes. They are now.

After the earthquake ceased, there was widespread fear in our village that the whole island might sink. In hindsight, that was not possible. Nothing so calamitous occurred that would cause a huge portion of the island to slide off and become submerged. As villagers, we were knowledgeable in navigating within our small world, not about tectonic plates and how they could impact our island. It should be noted that Vlahata was far enough away from the epicenter that although significant damage occurred, it was nothing like what occurred in Argostoli or Lixouri.

I recall one story of finding two women alive in Argostoli several days after the earthquake. They were found under the rubble of their home. The rescuers were surprised to find them alive after such a lengthy period. They survived their ordeal by eating raw potatoes. The liquid and the meat of the potatoes were apparently enough to sustain them until they were discovered. To this day, we still get the occasional earthquake. But the homes are now built to withstand severe earthquake activity.

In fact, when an earthquake occurs, eerie as it sounds, when it happens and I am visiting, it is comforting to me. Case in point, an earthquake occurred in the mid-1990s, when I was walking in the business section of Argostoli. It was measured at 4.5 on the Richter scale. For a moment, all the buildings wilted like trees and within that same second went back to their proper position. I smiled and thought as if the earthquake was a living, breathing entity. "*Bagasa* (son of a gun), is this your way of welcoming me back?" And it was then and now a feeling of euphoria. This was Kefalonia's way of reminding me to not forget her. Kefalonia has nothing to worry about. Her essence is forever embedded in my heart and soul. I am certain this is quite common for us whose origins are from there.

In a Wikipedia article, I was happily surprised that a video taken in Argostoli showed an old priest with a white beard and a short stature, wearing the customary clothing expected of priests while in public. He was speaking to a foreign newscaster about the devastation. Next to the priest was a handsome young man with curly brown hair. To my pleasant surprise, this was my father's youngest brother, George. At the time of that video, Uncle George would have been thirty years old.

When I last saw our uncle, he was in his seventies, still sharp but suffering from cancer, which eventually ended his life. I always made a point to see him when I traveled to Europe on business and then to Kefalonia. Because of his deteriorating condition, he had asked to see me, and I am so glad I went. After we hugged and wished him well, I left to return to the States. As I was hugging him, I looked at my wonderful aunt a few feet away, looking at us with tears, as if acknowledging the end for this good man was near. Sadly, not too much later, this came to pass.

Uncle George and the siblings who I was fortunate to meet were very kind and humble people—my kind of people. The ones who I met Stateside or in Greece were Eleni, Dionisis, Antelini, Spiro, and Gerasimoula (Mimoula).

I knew my uncle Spiro from the moment I arrived in Chicago with my family. This is because he, along with my father and their cousins Mihali and Koula, arrived in the United States in the early to mid-1950s. All came on the same boat and were brought to America by their uncle Gerasimos Pavlatos and his wife, Stella.

Uncle Dionisios lived in Panama. He was brought there by Uncle Basilios Kourouklis. I met Uncle Dionisi and family the one and only time in the early 1970s, when he traveled to Chicago to visit his brothers—my father (Gerasimo), Spiro, and George. Uncle George first lived in Panama by invitation of his brother Dionisi. In time, with his family, he migrated to Chicago. By all accounts and measure, Uncle Dionisi was an excellent family man and a good and supportive brother.

Prior to the earthquake, Kefalonia was a vibrant economy with approximately 125,000 inhabitants—this despite the devastation of World War II and the Civil War of 1946 to 1949. After the earthquake, 100,000 or so natives left and went to other countries seeking their fortune. The United States, Germany, England, and Australia were the principal beneficiaries of this diaspora. To date, Kefalonia has not totally recovered from the catastrophe created by the earthquake. For example, after all these years, the population of Kefalonia approximates no more than 40,000 inhabitants. A significant drop from the pre-earthquake period: and probably 15,000 of these are immigrants from adjoining countries seeking employment or refuge. Many were from Albania, and others were from Russia and Bulgaria. Others were war refugees from the Middle East's seemingly endless conflicts.

I believe this to be a net positive for Kefalonia and for Greece. I am guessing that based on history and proximity, Albanians, Serbians, and Bulgarians should already carry a decent amount of Greek DNA. More importantly, fresh blood is good for diversity and growth of a nation. Just look at the American model. How many impactful scientists and successful individuals have origins from different countries and races who have measurably enhanced the quality of life in America? Way too many to list.

There is no foreseeable engine that will bring impactful number of expatriates back to Kefalonia; perhaps the refugees from the Middle East or other troubled areas will fill the gap and assimilate. If from Islamic countries, it may create problems for some locals. Religions in general can nurture unjustified and dangerous fanaticism, especially when things get tough. That is also true for ethnophobia. In my opinion, extremists on both sides have and will always be on the wrong side of history. And history is replete with senseless, irrational, and unconscionable cruelty and carnage from both. On the bright side, it appears as the world becomes more affluent, it also is becoming a gentler and more understanding place. And due to modern technology, which is constantly improving exponentially, it is getting to be a smaller and smaller world. It is a good thing that we are planning to colonize Mars in the near future and establish an ongoing presence on the moon.

As previously noted, a small section of Argostoli sank under water. Unfortunately, it appears this section included the building that held all the records of native Kefalonians from previous generations. This was advised to me by my late uncle Dionisios Kourouklis, the protopresbyter of Panagia (Virgin Mary), the church in Frangata. This was the church where my parents and other ancestors attended, got baptized and married. Father Dionisios was first cousins with my mother.

With this destruction, census records were lost, which makes it difficult to go back in time and build a substantive family tree of all the branches of our family. Thankfully, with the help of my cousin Nikki Proutsos, I have been able to go as far back as 1871 on the paternal side; and 1880 on the maternal side. Perhaps the church records in Frangata and/or Athens' Census Bureau may have this information. Additional research is required to determine what information may still be available to expand our family tree.

Prior to his passing on December 3, 2019, Father Dionisios, even in his late eighties was mentally and physically sharp. This is not unique for villagers—people who live a country life and make their own fresh foods that are grown and raised on their land, thus eliminating all the processing, preservatives, and chemicals incorporated in our daily meals that as city dwellers in America we poison our bodies and minds with. Empirical evidence suggests village folks tend to live longer and healthier lives with lucid minds well into old age. In the States, long-term care is a serious consideration for many over sixty. I am not so sure I do not fit into the last category. Hopefully, I will have passed before that ever happens!

I was planning to return in the near future and see our uncle, probably for the last time. It was obvious that he was rapidly aging since Phyllis and I last saw him. With his passing, we lost a good relative and an industrious and benevolent priest. May his memory be eternal, and may it continue to bless all that knew and loved him. In our last visit, Father Dionisis gifted us with a beautiful Bible, which he personally, with his written comments, blessed and wished us well.

We had a donkey, Kapsoulas, and a much-loved, smart, and protective dog named Dickie. Kapsoulas was probably not a fan of mine. One day, he was eating hay and I must have been annoying. Kapsoulas grabbed me by my back with his teeth and threw me as far as he could. I never bothered him again. I must have been four or five at that time.

Dickie and Kapsoulas were buddies. When Ted, Kapsoulas, and Dickie were going to work, Kapsoulas would allow Dickie to walk between his legs as they passed the house owned by family friends, the Minetaiee. They owned three or four dogs. Dogs are by nature territorial; also, this group, did not like Dickie. To protect himself, Dickie would walk between Kapsoulas' legs. Every time this pack tried to attack him, Kapsoulas would kick them and protect his friend. In the appendix, there is a picture of Ted on top of Kapsoulas and next to them Dickie. Ted was probably fourteen to fifteen years old. It is a picture of the three friends going to work! Each had each other's back.

Dickie was very protective of our family. When Tony and Ted would argue and almost come to blows, Dickie would grab one of them by the pants and try to pull him away. As the youngest, Dickie spent a good amount of time with me. I remember an adult friend of the family named Bobby (shortened from Haralambos) would tease me for fun; he liked me. The breakdown of the name suggests its origin is *hara* (happiness) and *lambos* (shine). "Bobby" would get on his knees and profusely beg for forgiveness for stealing my "tsouvali" (sack) full of hay. Thinking he was serious, I would ask him in my low, stern voice, "*Yiati ore' mou pires to tsouvali* (Why you took my sack of hay)?" Still on his knees, Bobby would profusely apologize and beg for forgiveness. Unforgiving, I would tell Dickie to bite him. Thankfully, Dickie had more sense than me.

My mother told me that I walked at seven months. For years, I did not believe this to be possible or true. But when I started visiting Kefalonia in the mid- to late 1980s, accompanied by my own family, our next-door neighbor Angeliki (bouli'nena) confirmed this. Angeliki was younger than my mother by probably ten to fifteen years. In 1950 she and my mom both gave birth at about the same time. My mom had me, and Angeliki had Dionisi. My mother was forty-five years old and after having seven children, could not produce any or enough milk to feed me. She would hand me to Angeliki who would provide me with some of her abundant milk. Angeliki swore by all that is important and holy to her that I was seven months and just wearing an underwear. She advised that after I had my fill of milk, I pushed away, got off her lap, and started walking on rocks with no shoes on. I must have been strong, and strong willed then. How things have changed in my old age.

I realize this is hard to believe, but that is what I heard. My spouse, Phyllis, was with me and witnessed this discussion. Because of this neighborly kindness, every time I traveled to Greece, and as long as she was alive, I would visit Angeliki. I would gift her about fifty dollars and bring pastries to thank her for her kindness in giving me her milk when I was a baby. My mother advised that Angeliki was very beautiful as a young woman. When I met her in her later years, she was round and weathered by time. Still, her mind was sharp, and she was very kind. Most importantly, she was beloved by her family.

Angeliki was staying in the same house she lived all her life with her son Nikolaos, Xanthoula (daughter-in-law), and their three children: Spiro, Gerasimos, and their daughter, Angeliki. It is well constructed and well maintained by her second child, Nick. Her son Dionisios, who was the same age as me and both drank his mother's milk, died young of a drug overdose. I never saw Dionisi after we left for America. I did visit Kefalonia in the early 1970s, but I believe by that time he had left for the merchant marines. Dionisi was a very handsome young man with a nickname (*kouklos*—that is, doll). Apparently, he acquired the drug habit in the merchant marines, and that eventually killed him. This happened(s) to many young folk born in a village who left for better opportunities. Innocent of life's iniquitous, dark worldly ways, instead of fortune, they often found death or worse.

His death tortured his mother until her death. I cannot comprehend the severity of this pain, which stayed with her for the remainder of her life. Sadly, whenever she would see me, it would remind her of her Dionisi, and she would be in tears. I would try to comfort her but what words of comfort can one say for one that has lost so much and so dear to her? Even now, thinking of this fine person and her loss saddens me. I hope she has found the peace she so richly deserved.

A childhood memory recalls that Nick and Dionisi (Boulinae) were throwing rocks at my sister Kathy and Mom, which necessitated them taking cover in our little shack. Their house was no more than 150 feet upslope from our wooden shack. When I saw what was going on, I went out and started throwing rocks at them in retaliation; they stopped and went into their home. Kathy advised that the rock fight was triggered by an argument between our mothers.

Despite the two being good friends, when you live so close for so long, even between friends, tempers can flare, especially in those difficult times.

Zografia

The Kefalonians are by nature mischievous pranksters and jokers. To my wife's irritations, I am one of them. But this is not about me. It is about the most famous Kefalonian prankster I have known or heard of—Zografia Minetos. I must have been about five or six when she performed this outlandish prank.

The Minetaiee were good friends of our family and good neighbors. Zografia was the matriarch of the Mineteiee. She, like the rest of the people of that era had many kids, albeit I do not recall how many. I am certain she had at least four; two of each gender. *Zografia* implies "picture" in Greek, meaning she was beautiful as a picture. Zografia is a derivative of *Zografos*, which in English means "painter," as in an artist who paints pictures of people or nature, etc. I do not recall Zografia at all, so I cannot confirm or deny if the name fits the person. But, as you will see, she was obviously a character.

It is my understanding that this was the time of the year when priests would stop by the house and bless one's animals. The Matriarch of the Minetaiee clan called on the village priest and advised him that her *kounelaki* (bunny) was ailing. Could he please stop by the house and bless it? Dutifully, the following day, the priest walked to Zografia's house and politely asked, "My child, where can I find the infirmed animal?" Zografia took the local cleric behind her barn. Looking around and not finding the rabbit, the priest, baffled, asked again, "*Zografia mou, pou eine to kounelaki sou* (Dearest Zografia, where is your bunny)?"

With pretentious sincerity, which in reality was total insincerity, Zografia looked the beguiled priest straight in his eyes and slowly lifted the front of her dress. By this time, the shocked priest's eyes must have been wide open. The prankster showed him that she was not wearing any undergarments and said in a calm and mischievous voice the following immortalized words: "Here is my *kounelaki*, Father. Can you please bless it?" I'm not sure what he said, if anything, but I am guessing it was not pretty. And I am comfortable in stating that he left as quickly as his legs allowed him to and most likely continued crossing himself, asking for God's mercy for a depraved soul.

Zografia could not stop laughing and was proud of her audacious prank. The whole village was made aware, and all were laughing. I hope that included her husband and children. Zografia must have been about fifty years of age at the time of this prank. It was so legendary and bold that after seventy-plus years I still remember it, and I still laugh. Thank you for the memories, Zografia mou!

I remember walking in the fields and picking wild asparagus and bringing them to my mom to cook them for me with scrambled eggs. On one of those walks, I found a circular house made of hay that was approximately a foot and a half wide, with a hardened mud top. It was made by an animal, and as it appeared firm, I jumped on it. Every time I jumped, I heard squealing.

After a couple of times, not knowing what it was, I cautiously got off. Then I saw a large hare run out as if its life depended on it. I felt relief, as it was a hare and not a dangerous or aggressive animal.

My childhood friends were primarily the boulinaee (Angeliki's) younger children. This included Nikolas (about two years older), Dionisis (my age), and Rebecca (about two years younger). Boulinos is the clan name, just as ours is Liguris. Their family name is Galiatsatos. The father's name was Spiros, or Boulinos. The father was a good man and respected within our community. I did not see much of him, and I recall he was sick and bedridden for a lengthy period.

Mr. Galiatsatos passed prior to our departure to America. I'm not certain the cause of death. I do know that he was sent, along with my brother-in-law Erotocritos, to Makronisos for six months. This island was chosen by the government to hold for a period, for "reeducation purposes," suspected Communist sympathizers who participated in the Greek Civil War (1946-1949). I assume indoctrination and probably tough love was the primary goal of this confinement. At least one person who was there advised that severe beatings were not uncommon. It does not appear to have been easy for those that were sent there. Probably, just the opposite. I believe both sides were guilty of such behavior. Literature suggests the Communists, at least in the beginning, were more aggressive with bad intentions, such as preemptive killing of the opposition. This is documented history.

It is well known in all of Greece, that Kefalonian's are not only a bit "too" high-strung but also blasphemous to an extreme. For the Kefalonians, cursing is basically a hobby—a stranger would be amazed in their creativity for cursing and verbal abuse. I am not certain that these diatribes have a bottom. Still, they are harmless. Just blowing steam off, and sometimes funning between friends. When Kefalonian's get upset, they initiate their sacrilegious tirades, by using the name of Jesus, Saint Gerasimos (our patron saint), the Virgin Mary, Saint Spiridon, Saint Dionisios, etc., against the object of their anger. Still, these malevolent sounding declarations are usually harmless but can continue for quite a while. Usually, after the run out of saints' names.

I last witnessed such a tirade from my old neighbor and friend, Nikola. It was "siesta time," when most Greeks in Greece, nationally, enjoy their afternoon nap. Nick's goat must have been disturbed by something or just got tired of being tied to a tree for hours, on a hot, humid summer day. As a result, the goat would not stop bleeping. Nick eventually came out of his siesta, and in the loudest, most vehement expression of displeasure, he swore at the goat a continuous onslaught of anything and everything that was holy and unholy. Cursing the poor goat by calling out every saint, Christ, the Virgin Mary, and others, he even cursed the goat's mother and father, even its owner! And any other ill wish or blasphemy that he could think of; including that the poor goat die a cruel death and more.

This abusive attack lasted for a while. Of course, Nick was just letting out steam and this tirade, as aggressive as it sounded, was harmless. At the end of the day, Nick loved his goat. Still, I was truly amazed and amused by Nick's creativity and commitment for "retribution."

I was sitting quietly and enjoying the gorgeous view of our gulf from Tony's second-floor balcony. Nick did not notice me. Shortly after, and sounding "concerned," I mischievously interjected, "*Nikola mou, eine ola entaxi* (My friend, Nikolas, *is everything okay*)?" Nick did not even look back. He got the jab, probably cursing me under his breath and calling me names. I am certain *malakas* would have been one of the preferred adjectives he would have crowned me with. This adjective is one of the most often used word in modern Greek! It is double-sided and can be used menacingly with anger and ill intent; or, believe it or not, as an expression of friendship and affection. Still, it is recommended that for self-preservation it be not used unless speaking to a good friend.

Although Dionisis was my age, my memories suggest that I hung out principally with Nick and even Rebeka more than Dionisi. When I last saw Rebeka, she was a beautiful, measured young lady, married and a university graduate. Of the four kids, she was the only one that went to a university. It was probably rare in that era that a daughter went to a university and not a son. My guess is that none of the boys wished to pursue higher education and Rebeka did.

I remember taking turns with Nick and Dionisi throwing rotten eggs at rocks and then paying the price by catching a whiff of that odious odor. At that time, we thought it was fun!

When I was about five or six, I remember climbing up on a tree to catch a Cicada. I wore shorts and somehow a bee got in my underwear. The bee stung me on one of my testicles. That testicle got very puffy and uncomfortable for at least a week. I suppose my brothers were making jokes about this painful incident. Although it hurt then, it is funny now. Thankfully, my privates eventually normalized, and the acquired luster was short-lived. Is it not an oxymoron that a week of suffering can be a lifelong good memory? And it was then, and it still is now.

I remember being about five or six and going to the beach by myself for a swim. The walk to the beach is not far. It is a downslope with winding roads as one would expect. When you are about three American blocks from the shore, the road flattens to almost the level of the beach and narrows to a one lane road. In the spring and summer, it is verdant, especially on the right side toward the village, with thick foliage due to a decent number of springs located in this area. Therefore, one can expect snakes to be lurking, and one must be careful where they walk. As a rule, snakes try to avoid humans and only become aggressive if they are surprised or are protecting their young.

After the swim, as I entered this path to return home, on my left side I heard what sounded like dry leaves crackling, as if something were following me. Due to the thickness of vegetation, which was about seven feet away parallel to me, I could not see the cause of this noise. I was scared but did not panic. I stopped to look and heard a threatening noise that sounded like a whistle. I continued walking, and as I walked, I kept hearing the crackling of leaves with the rhythm of a snake movement. When I would stop, this ominous whistle would begin again. This continued for about three or four times. After a bit, as I was exiting this area, whatever was following me stopped.

I can only surmise it was a snake and probably springtime when their babies hatch and hence was being protective. If springtime, not certain why the leaves would crack unless they were last year's leftovers. Irrespective, I was lucky that I was not attacked. The snakes in Kefalonia although a good number are poisonous and deadly, are not known to whistle. Instead, they hiss. Still, based on a discussion I had with Kathy, it was probably an ohia, a very deadly snake. I share this info because Kathy was once threatened by an ohia, and she said the hissing sounded like a whistle. Perhaps I was sufficiently traumatized that my mind transformed the hiss into a whistle. A snake that whistles truly does exist. In the English language, it is named "dice snake" and it is not poisonous. It is not indigenous to Kefalonia. It can be found in Crete and perhaps other parts of Greece.

The consensus is there are not as many snakes now in Kefalonia as in the 1950s. It appears that with the extensive buildup of Vlahata and Kefalonia in general, there is not enough prey for food. For example, we used to have significant flocks of swallows. Now swallows have measuredly decreased. This negatively impacts the snake population of Kefalonia. Although like almost all animals, snakes have a purpose and place on this earth, I cannot say this saddens me.

I remember our mother taking tomatoes, mashing them, and putting them in sacks to produce *coserva* (tomato paste), also taking fish and smoking them.

My recollection is that it was a very agreeable taste. I remember my mother making and baking bread in our round oven that was outside, away from the house, probably made of mud and clay. I am certain she did this and more to prepare and have sufficient provisions to sustain the family in the winter and in general. That was the customary routine of women in our village.

There is a little incline above the beach where we would swim that has a little church. The rise is called Trapezaki. This, I assume, is because it reminds one of a table. Recall that *Trapezaki*, in Greek, means little table. There were celebrations held at that little church on certain holidays days. Perhaps there still are. One day, two of my friends and I were playing on top of Trapezaki. All three were about five years of age. I turned over a small rock and saw a small black snake, which I proceeded to kill. Unbeknown to me, this is the least aggressive but most deadly snake in Kefalonia. It is called Konaki. The saying is that it has such a lethal bite that if you are bitten, "three steps and you are dead." Ted advised that one of his friend's fathers was bitten and subsequently died from the bite of a Konaki.

Another snake episode was on the main road to Argostoli, Kefalonia's capital city. We were headed toward Argostoli but I do not recall our destination. There was a festival and my friends and I were walking with the rest of the villagers. Right after the *magalo yiro* (big turn, which turned out to be a small turn when I grew up and saw it again), there was ground dug up by the side of the mountain on the northside of the road. It was about six to eight feet deep and about five feet wide. Its composition was white gravel, used for construction projects. At the bottom of this pit appeared to be someone's feces.

The joker in me said to my friends, "I am going to jump down and crap on top of that dump." Luckily, before jumping, on the opposite side of the "dump," the mountainside, I looked down and noticed a small round hole near the bottom of the pit and froze. It was not someone's feces. It was a curled snake; the dangerous *ohia*, poisonous and aggressive when cornered. It could spell death or at minimum, a very serious injury if the bite was not treated on a timely basis.

We threw a few good-size rocks and killed the ohia. I recall an adult male partook in the rock throwing. I assume he wanted to make certain the snake was dead. Every time it was hit, it would hiss and prepare to attack. But the poor snake had no place to run and could not vertically jump or climb such a height. In hindsight, the snake probably moved to the far end of the mountain to get into a shaded area, as it was hot and around noon.

Jumping is supposed to be for another well-known Kefalonian poisonous snake. This snake is called saitari (jumper)! I have been told the saitari can jump as far as ten feet while attacking; however, anatomically, it does not seem to be possible for a ground snake to perform such a feat. Recently I questioned two credible sources: Ted and my brother-in-law Totos. Still, in his early nineties, Toto has a very good memory. A saitari delivers less poisonous than an ohia' or konaki but is larger in size and more aggressive. Totos advised that although he has not witnessed an attack by a saitari, it jumps about five to ten feet when attacking. My brother Ted is of a similar opinion. I'm not certain how it jumps, but again anatomy would suggest its jump is not anywhere ten feet in height. Perhaps no higher than face level, probably much less. Still, I need to expand my query about this infamous snake to verify or disprove.

I remember walking with my mother and the rest of the siblings around the *megalo giro* (large turn) toward home and all of us singing popular songs of that time. One that I vividly remember is a song from a singer name Vembo. She was a popular female singer, probably in her forties at the time of this song. The lyrics were about a man named Lia'—short for Ilias. As the song goes, the singer would do anything for Lia'. Part of the song says, "*Yia to Lia' 'ehoun gini koutsobolia' … kai yia to gustomou viagzo to boustomou* (For Ilias, there has been much gossip about he and I, and for my pleasure I would take off my bustier, which melts 'Lia,' and so on and so forth)." Although it sounds a bit risqué, it did not come across as such to us. We saw it as a fun and witty song. It was a nice piece of music. And in its time, very popular, as was the singer. Of course, being named Ilia's and being the youngest, my family could not resist teasing me.

Another popular song that was a big hit and *manggiko* (a bit of rebel in it) was "*stou yialou to votsalakia kathonde ta kavourakia* (By the pebbles of the shore sitting there are baby crabs). It was about a Mrs. Crab finding a new lover, going to Athens, and partying, while papa crab tended to the poor baby crabs who were crying for their mama by the pebbles near the shore. It was a big hit then, and on occasion the song is still played on the radio. It has a lively and enjoyable tune and fun lyrics. Clearly, the song is a metaphor for an illicit love affair. I have this song on a disk and still enjoy hearing it.

Another wonderful song at that time and probably to this day is a beautiful love serenade that we would sing while walking back home on the same road was "*Dio prasina matia*" (two green eyes). Essentially, it was a young man singing about a beautiful green-eyed girl and seeing her drove him crazy with affection for her. I still recall a couple of phrases of this beautiful serenade and occasionally play it on my piano. Full disclosure, I play the piano very average at best. On the plus side, I do not charge for my services; the listeners suffering is more than enough!

The Planned Agreement to Adopt

My mother advised that when I was a baby my godparents Gerasimos and Rodessa Koutrohoi wanted to adopt me as they could not have children. Because of the hard times brought forth by the recently ended Civil War, my father was willing; I understand that my godparents, with hands extended, where encouraging me to go with them. I assume I was a year or so old. As I started walking toward them, my mother could not accept the loss of her child and put a stop to this plan. She categorically stated that this request cannot and will not be allowed. Because of her decision, both families became estranged and never met or spoke again. So sad for both. Clearly, my godparents were very disappointed and apparently must have thought they had consummated a deal.

Prior to the estrangement, I was baptized by my godparents. My mother wanted to name me Peter, after her first husband who was killed in Panama in the 1930s. In a surprising move, my godfather changed that at the altar. He named me Ilias, after his late father. It was his right under the Orthodox ecclesiastic etiquette. For the record, Peter is a nice name; but I like Ilias better—much better!

Going back to the subject of adoption, I often wonder how I would have taken the adoption, should my parents allow the adoption to consummated. I think not very well for many reasons. There is something innate between family of the same blood. I am convinced my godparents would have been great parents. And as a youth, I would have been happy and living quite comfortably. But as I would have grown to maturity, I would have asked questions and received answers that would have made it difficult for me to accept. You see, nothing is thicker than blood. Nothing is more important than blood. And as much as you may love and care for your magnificent adoptive parents, nothing makes you feel better than your own blood—even if they are a pain to live and be with. At the end of day, I would have felt unloved, unwanted, and betrayed by those who made me. Even if well intended, it is hard to imagine anything harder to accept than this. Thank you, Mom, for stopping a well-intended but ill-thought-out decision, with so many ramifications, and none of them desirable! Please don't misunderstand me. Adoption for so many is a blessing. But knowing myself as I do, if avoidable, not for me.

After high school in 1969, and at eighteen years old, I decided to vacation at my place of birth, Greece. It was my first trip back since departing for America. With my mother's urging, I made a point to visit my godparents' whom I never met, except as a one-year-old. Their house had a gate at the entrance near the main road. There were cement stairs going to the house, which equally divided the cultivated part of the plot with fruits and vegetables. I opened the gate and saw a woman in her fifties, carefully eyeing me as I walked down the stairs. The distance from road to house was roughly one hundred feet, with about 50 percent downslope to the one-story house. Her first name was Rodessa. As her name implies, she was beautiful, very kind, and likeable.

I said in Greek, "*Kiria* (Mrs.) Koutrohois?" She replied, "*Malista*" (This is "yes," but in a respectful manner. The common way of saying "yes" is *ne*).

I then asked playfully, and making eye contact, if she knew who I was. She stared at me, carefully studied me, and said in Greek, "*Oxi Kiriai* (No sir)."

Again, I asked her to take another look, and playfully I turned sideways and straight a couple of times.

She looked at me with kindness and uncomfortably replied, "Forgive me, sir. I do not know you."

"*Eime o Ilias* (I am Ilias)!" I exclaimed and smiled.

With tears, she lovingly replied, "*Ilia mou, eise esi* (My Ilias, is it you)?"

We hugged and kissed as a mother and son. She then called my godfather to come home quickly. I met him, and we were all very happy to finally meet.

I stayed with my godparents for two days. I helped my godfather who was industrious, even in his elder hears, with minor chores that needed tending and helped him clean up their yard and paint the flowerpots white. White has always been a preferred color in Greece; blue, possibly second. The flowerpots were good-size and round. If my recollection is accurate, each horizontally elongated stair had a flowerpot. The flowerpot containers were metallic, probably tin. The walkways where rectangular in shape. Each step measured about four or five feet in horizontal length; about six inches vertically.

My godfather advised that he first became good friends with my father when they were both working tirelessly and endlessly, to dig and extend underground lines in roads around and up and down the mountainside. I believe the wiring was to bring electricity to Kefalonia in places where it was lacking. Based on his description, the work must have been a very trying and strenuous. They were almost always dying of thirst; and there where were times where heat exhaustion was almost too much to bear. There is a decent amount of fertile land in Kefalonia. Nevertheless, much of Kefalonia is rock foundation with little dirt covering. It must have been very tiring but important work that would enable Kefalonia to join the modern world and to do well in the post–Civil War era.

My godfather enjoyed eating crumbled pieces of feta cheese, mixed, in oil, and Herbs that complimented this tasty dish. This delicacy, he advised was called *preza*. He would always ask me to join him and would say in Greek, "*Fae Liamou preza* (Eat, my Ilias preza)." It was too tasty to refuse. Most importantly, it was offered with affection by people who felt as if they just found a long-lost son.

As they were well to do, my godparents had several godchildren. I was their first. As I was preparing to say my goodbyes, they showed me properties they owned and with moist eyes, asked me to take the best one for myself. From what I saw, they owned a decent amount of fertile land in prime locations from where they lived. I was happy for them. I thanked them for their kindness and generous offer. But since I lived in America,

I noted that any gift of value to me would go to waste. I recommended they give the property to another godchild who was local. All I wanted was their love. And both ways it was unconditional and in abundance.

I remember, as a boy, walking to a monastery located in the town of Sísia to a celebrate a saint. The clergy and laity church leaders would carry banners, icons, and other church relics in the procession. It was a very long walk from our village. I think if I would attempt this walk today, being old, raised in the city and grossly out of shape, I would probably die from exhaustion. But as a youth, I do not recall it being an issue. My niece Noula Angelos, a history aficionado in her own right, advised it was named after Saint Francis of Assisi, a Catholic friar who visited Kefalonia and prayed where the monastery was built. Friar Francis was later canonized a saint.

In medieval times, the monastery was an impressive edifice and well known. The all-masonry monastery was founded by Saint Francis around AD 1300. It was originally Catholic, but in time it became Orthodox. It was destroyed by earthquakes, with the latest being the earthquake of 1953. A new monastery was built nearby. I never saw it but would be surprised if the new monastery comes anywhere near the grandeur and quality of the original.

In AD 1300, I believe Kefalonia was a protectorate of Venice. I say this because the Venetians and French Crusade double-crossed Byzantium and ransacked and pilfered it in 1204. Allegedly, their sole objective was to free Jerusalem from Saracen control but stopped at Byzantium to rest, resupply, and then travel to the Holy Land.

After seeing such wealth and opulence, apparently the crusaders reconsidered their options and decided, in God's name, to rape and pillage the Beacon of Christianity. In fact, the Pope after meeting with the crusaders, famously and shamelessly blessed this evil deed and stated that "going to Byzantium was tantamount to going to Jerusalem!" For good measure, the French rode their horses into Saint Sophia, killed whoever they could find, and then urinated on the altar. This pillaging, killing, and destruction caused by their "allies" in Christ resulted in a steep and irreversible decline of Byzantium. Venice became the new superpower of its time. As a result, it had access to all Greek islands, including Kefalonia, which they officially annexed in AD 1500.

Returning our story to modern times, when we were all married with kids, I had the pleasure to go down by the beach at Sísia with my brother Tony. Never been there before. Tony wanted me to enjoy the waters right below the monastery. He thought them special. It was an enjoyable swim, especially since I was swimming and reminiscing with my brother, who loved me enough to take the time and show me a place he especially enjoyed. I believe I now understand why. Saint Francis of Assisi must have also swam there and wanted his brother to enjoy the blessings the Saint brought to these waters; and blessed I have been in so many ways. Antoni mou, thank you for your thoughtfulness and love. Although you have left us, I hope you know it is reciprocated, and your memory never forgotten.

When I was about four years old, I had a pet baby goat, and it would follow me wherever I went. This goat and I became close. One day, because of our extreme poverty, my parents advised that they sold the goat, and I had to give it up. I remember being in tears and telling them not to do this. I loved that goat! Somewhere in our discussions, emphatically gesturing and by mistake, I hit one of its little horns, which resulted in it falling off. In our late adult years, speaking with my brother Ted, the baby goat was the offspring of a female goat that he and Tony received from the government. If a family met a certain threshold of poverty, they were entitled to receive a female goat. Ted advised that productive female goats usually produce three or four offspring. Those that did usually have good-size breasts. The goat they were given had small breasts. Villagers who were there first and chose the preferred goats were laughing at the selection. Two young boys who went a little too late. Still one offspring is better than none.

Our donkey Kapsoulas ate grass that was poisonous and died. Donkeys were not cheap and important for the work we did as farmers—carrying goods to the market, etc. My brother Ted, who was Kapsoula's caretaker, was devasted. We took our beloved donkey on a two-wheel cart that was big enough to haul him and tossed him in a huge crevice that was used, among other things, to dispose dead animals. The dumpsite was away from our village toward Sísia on the east side of the main road that connected our village to other villages. That was a significant loss to our family. Donkeys were the animal version of a modern-day pickup truck used to convey goods.

I remember a one-man strongman show once came to Vlahata. The villagers gathered in the main part of the town to witness his demonstration of strength. There was a huge round wooden pole on the ground. It was the type of pole that appeared to be used for telephone lines. It appeared heavy and long. As very young kids, we were impressed to witness this strongman able to push this log around with ease, using one leg while talking to us. Most of the village was there.

The strongman made an impression on me and my friend, Nick (Boulinos). Primarily in respect to one demonstration he performed. He nailed three or four nails, seemingly identical to those used in construction projects into a plank of wood. With his bare teeth, he was able to break them off. We both saw this, and when we went home we tried to emulate the feat. Much as we tried duplicating this prodigious accomplishment, we could not. Thankfully, we did not lose any teeth!

I remember a festival called Mascara (Mask). Males and females of all ages would dress up in customs, and they would dance. One dance was called Kantriles. They would dance, and as you see couples in the Old West dancing, with a dance director calling the partners to change partners, go to the left and to the right, etc. This was the same, except most of the directions were given in Italian. I assume the use of Italian was because Kefalonia was ruled by Venice for a long period of time-roughly three hundred years! In the same festival, another dance included holding long, various colored yarn about an inch in width, all the same length and all tied to a pole in the middle that would be static and be held by an individual. The dancers would dance around and as they did, by the end of the dance, the material would be totally wrapped around the pole. It was a beautiful and scenic sight to see.

I saw this same dance duplicated when my son, George, was very young and was a part of a versatile Greek dance troupe sponsored by the Saint Athanasios Church. It was founded and run for many years by the late Dr. Michael Kontos; his wife, Eva; and their children, Gregory and Ellena. In their prime, they were magnificent dance instructors and a tremendous benefit to the youth of our community.

I dubbed Dr. Kontos the "Homer" of the dance troupe. Just like Homer, who through poetry empowered the Doric Greeks by educating them of their illustrious history and heritage, Dr. Kontos similarly, by teaching and educating our youth of our traditional old-world dances with corresponding customs, made our youth proud of their Hellenic Heritage. These beautiful traditional Greek dances originated from all over Greece, including Kefalonia, which our son George was the lead for our island's most famous dance, called the "Balo." All four richly deserved our gratitude and more.

During the Mascara festival, as the festival's name implies, villagers would put on masks and clothing. Guys and girls were permitted to change clothes and dress up as the opposite sex, including lipstick and dresses and vice versa. Tony shared that at the last Mascara before departing for America he was dressed as a girl with lipstick, and one of his friends was his partner. It sounded like a lot of fun. But I must admit, being raised in America and watching lots of John Wayne movies, I would have trouble dressing up as a girl. But then again, you must be very comfortable within your own skin to take such liberties in dress and presentation.

When my father came to America in 1954, after settling down a bit, he sent the family monies and gifts. This included a gift for me. I must have been about four or five. He sent me a toy monkey with a drum. When its metallic key was turned, the monkey beat the drum. For us village boys of similar age, we gazed in wonder at this magnificent toy! For a time, I felt special. Most importantly, our father was able to send monies for us to build a home, and we did. No more sleeping on dirt or in inclement weather!

Seeking a better life for their families, my father and his younger brother, Spiro, left for America a few years prior to our departure. Due to World War II, the subsequent brutality of the Civil War, as well as the significant suffering compounded by the earthquake of 1953, it was common for Greeks and other nationalities living in poverty who were able to leave their homeland in search of a better life. America, Canada, Germany, and Australia were the principle beneficiaries of this diaspora. Most immigrants planned to stay in the new country for a short period, with an objective of making a sufficient amount of funds to allow them to return and live comfortably in their native land.

Unfortunately, that usually was not the norm; it was the exception. Most of the immigrants became Americanized, Germanized, etc. They stayed and raised children. At some point they assimilated. Most made and continue to make positive contributions to their adopted countries.

For the record, I see the world as one race. Through thick or thin, we are all in this together in our spaceship called Mother Earth. We all have our biases and demons. Best we can do is recognize and control them. I try. It is not easy, but usually I succeed. Also, although my mind is American and, due to my vocation, strongly influenced by global affairs, I can almost guarantee my soul will always be Greek, with ancient Greek the dominant portion. I will always feel the pain as well as nobleness of my ancestors. I need to! This way, I hope to never forget who I am and where I came from!

I remember a song my mother would sing to me, "*Anthesmeni agmidalia.*" This is a very well-known, old serenade, *candatha*. It is still popular and sung in the islands of the Ionian Sea. The words are beautiful. It compares a young lady to an *agmidalia* (almond tree) in full blossom. As interpreted by many, including my mother, the poem implies that a young man left his village and went abroad to a distant land to seek his fortune. The song continues to imply that it took many years for this person to make his fortune and the years passed. When he returned, he found his beloved old with white hair, reminiscent of a blossomed almond tree.

At least this is how my mother explained it to me. I am certain she missed our father immensely. I researched this song and found it has a rich and interesting history; however, it was written with a different intent. In the late 1800s, a young poet went to Germany for higher education. After his schooling was completed, he returned home. One day, through the kitchen window, he saw his sixteen-year-old cousin and her friend playing in their yard. At one point, the girl playfully shook the almond tree, and she was filled with white buds. The girl was dusting off the buds from her hair and shoulders and other parts of her body. The young man, in his early twenties and an already accomplished and published poet, got an immediate picture in his mind and wrote the aforementioned poem, which became one of the most famous and beloved songs of all Greece.

"Anthismeni Agmidalia" was written in 1882 by Georgios Drosinis; his cousin's name was Drosina Drosinis. As the story goes, soldiers who were fighting a war (probably the Bulgarians for disputed territory on the northeast side near Macedonia (pre-World War I), heard this poem, repeated it often, and someone put it to music.

In the Ionian Islands, which include Kefalonia, Ithaki, Zakynthos, Corfu, Paxi, Kythira, and Lefkada, candathes are still loved and played. This song is one of those that is and will continue to be a favorite of the candathorie.

As a young boy, before departing for America, we went up to Frangata to say goodbye to my paternal grandmother. I was about seven when I met her this one last time. Based on her date of birth, 1881, my grandmother must have been around eighty years of age. She was bedridden due to an infection in one leg that could not heal. Do not know the cause of the infection but unfortunately, it had to be tended and cleaned daily. This was a difficult chore for her and her two remaining daughters, Mimoula and Andelini who were her caretakers. Both were unmarried; Mimoula had a hunched back, probably by mishandling at birth.

Both sacrificed a great deal to be their mother's caregivers. My aunt Andelini who had no physical impairments and attractive as a young girl, probably sacrificed the most. My aunt Mimoula's very visible hunchback took away much from what was probably a beautiful girl in her prime. Irrespective, she appeared to have acclimated well and did not seem to hold a grudge or be ill-tempered due to her unfortunate impairment.

When I met both in 1971, they were very happy to meet me and *so* kind. I stayed with them for a couple of days. During my stay, I realized I had to get up very early to beat my kind and generous aunts to the street vendor from whom they would buy fresh produce to make our meals. On one of those days, I was able to get there just in time to intervene and pay. They did not like that and profusely objected and admonished me to never pay again. Nothing but beautiful memories from two sweet, kind, and loving human beings. I shall never forget their affection and generosity. So glad I met and spent time with my two angelic aunts!

I remember when I was about five or six years of age and annoying my brother Ted would get upset and rendered minor punishment. In one of those instances when I was punished, a sweet little girl about three with blond hair would come and tell me in Greek baby talk, "*Pame, louee, babee mou na figoume apo to kako leteri* (Come with me, my Louee Garbis, away from this mean Ted)." This cute little girl was my niece Kathy, firstborn of my eldest sister, Dina. She grew up in America to be a fine lady. She married a quality person in John Rousakis and has beautiful grandkids. Despite her lack of higher education, she landed a job at National Baking Company and has become a senior manager in key areas of this company.

A recollection I have as a child is that we harvested sea urchins and swallowed the insides. I recall them being tasty and a delicacy for us village boys. At one time there were many sea urchins. Now they are extremely rare, at least in the shallows. I guess the villagers ate them to extinction.

My brother Anthony was a very handsome young man. All my brothers were handsome, but as Tony was about sixteen or seventeen, he was basically a young, mature gentleman. He was tall, good-looking, and measured; he stood out.

Most of his closest friends were older and respected him as an equal. For example, Nikos Haralambatos (nicknamed Saitoula, like the snake that allegedly jumps), about twenty-five years of age; Andreas Kornelatos, thirty years of age. There were a few more, but I do not recall their names. And Anthony is no longer with us, so I cannot ask him.

There was a very nice woman, probably about seven or eight years older than Tony, who he was friends with—no obvious nefarious activities. On occasions when she would see me, she would give me candies. I now assume it was a benefit for being Tony's little brother. I recall her with long curly black hair, kind, thin, with a good-looking, agreeable face and on the shorter side. In my youth, she appeared beautiful.

Apparently, the father (Loukas Spiratos), whom I recall being of progressed age, on the tall side, skinny with white hair, was concerned about the ongoing interaction between his only child, a young woman of twenty-five, and Anthony, who was about sixteen or seventeen. Riri's mother had passed. Occasionally, you could hear the old man from a higher level near his house directing his voice toward the beach, loudly, with a bit of ominous nervousness, calling to his daughter, "*Riri! Oxi me ton Antoni* (Riri, not with Anthony)!" He was admonishing his daughter to come home and not hang around Antoni.

I remember Riri as a beautiful and kind person. But I cannot vouch for either's behavior. Anthony had eloquence, panache, and stature—and a young man of seventeen, mature beyond his young years and being involved with an older woman is not unheard of. Nevertheless, Andoni denied any involvement. I *think* I believe him. Riri was her shortened name. Rereeka was her full name.

CHAPTER 4

Commentaries of Relevant and Socially Impactful Topics

A Comparison of the Greek and American Civil Wars

Although the Greek Civil War started around 1943 while still under German-Italian occupation, the bloodiest part of the war took place between 1946 to the end of 1949. In that period alone, at least 149,000 people were killed. The Greek Civil War started slowly, with pockets of Communist sympathizers who had already begun killing those who posed a threat to their objective of turning Greece into a communist country. Although there were deaths, the number of dead from both sides are not clear for the years 1943 through 1945 period. Since I know of no verifiable figure for that period, I will not include fatalities suffered during that earlier era of the Civil War. As noted, the death toll picked up measurably between 1946 and 1949. The records suggest that this was a very personal, vicious, and bloody war. It pitted brother against brother, father against son, not unlike the American Civil War, but on a much smaller scale.

Comparing the American Civil War, and taking out the Black population, which was about 3.5 million, primarily in bondage, the

American white population in the Civil War era is estimated to have been about 27.5 million, as opposed to 7 million in Greece at the time of the Greek Civil War. The American casualties were estimated to be around 630,000. To make the losses comparable, I multiplied the Greek casualties by 3.93 (27.5/7) as a reasonable comparison of the impact the number of dead had on the nation. My simplistic analysis indicates that just for the 1946 to 1949 period, if the Greek population of this time were equal to that of the United States (27.5 million), 585,570 Greeks would have died as a result of the Civil War. This indicates the Greek Civil War, from a societal and economic standpoint, was probably as costly to Greece as the American Civil War was to America. Furthermore, if we were able to estimate those who were killed by the Communists in 1943 through 1945, probably more.

Although the Greek Civil War was disastrous and brutal, the American Civil War was far more brutal, bloodier, and due to the issue of human slavery, much more personal. I must also mention that Black men were allowed to join the Union army after Lincoln's Emancipation Proclamation Act of 1862. Records suggest over 179,000 Black soldiers entered the war, of which it is estimated that 40,000 died—30,000 due to infectious disease and 10,000 in battle. I have assumed that the total Black war casualties were similar to those of the Greek Civil War from 1943 to 1945 and therefore a wash. Because of this assumption, I decided to extract the Black population from the comparison. But make no mistake, the Black soldiers fought bravely and made a significant difference in the outcome of this pernicious war. They more than earned their freedom. As freedom should be an innate entitlement to all of humanity, the Black enslaved population of America should not have had to "earn" their liberty. But they did!

In conclusion, The American North fought for an ideology based on the premise that all people are created equal and deserve the right to live, prosper, and the pursuit of happiness. Furthermore, slavery is a vicious and odious aberration of reality, extremely cruel, and against our Christian and European values!

The Disturbing Issue of Slavery in America

So there is no mistake of how I feel about the enslavement of Blacks in the Antebellum South, please bear with me and close your eyes: Picture yourself as a Black man or woman who was a slave prior to emancipation.

You are as intelligent as the next white man or women and are endowed by God to have, like every other human being, normal, human feelings. Livestock is treated better than you and your family; you and yours are totally disrespected and denigrated. You are often callously abused in a myriad of cruel and creative ways by your "owner." The "masters," with pleasure, regularly remind you of everything they think you are not. To them, you are less than a beast of burden. Your wife and daughter(s) are raped at will by the master, his friends, or family members on the plantation. Your children, on a regular basis, are vilified and mentally abused, with the purpose of reenforcing, from a very young age, to think themselves less than human, with smaller brains and intellect. Your spouse and loved ones, without conscious consideration and a lack of humanity, sold as chattel to increase family wealth or to pay down debt. You want to badly but cannot fight back, because of the unimaginable suffering you and your family will experience at the hands of these vile humans if you do. How would you feel? What would you do if that happened to your child? We all know the answer.

For the record, not all slave owners were cruel and abusive. But this does not ameliorate the first sin of acceptance and implementation of slavery. This was and always will be an unforgivable sin! It is one thing to be a Black chief in Africa conquering and selling people of your race and color. Although totally wrong, the chief grew up in that environment and did not have our values. But the North American whites knew better—much better. They disregarded justice and humanity for the sake of comfort and greed. And this was supposed to be a Christian society with Christian values? So sad that we humans are probably the only species that can mold our logic to rationalize our means to justify our ends—hypocrisy must be our middle name. For the record, there were whites in the South who did not condone this ugly aberration of humanity. God bless them, and God bless the abolitionist John Brown, who, with his sons, sacrificed their lives for the abolition of this insidious and criminal institution. Most of all, God bless Abraham Lincoln for fighting the war that gave Black people their freedom!

The Plight of the Indigenous Americans

To get closer to the truth, it is said that you open one door and find ten more doors that require opening. This process can go on infinitely.

In time, with commitment, you might feel comfortable that your findings are reasonable. One example of "peeling the onion" in search of the truth can be found in American history. Starting from the time the Europeans landed at Jamestown, Virginia (1607), and their continued migrations westward with high intensity, as the expansion for land and wealth was in its heyday.

My findings suggest that in the early stages in their interface with the immigrants, most indigenous tribes were hospitable, conciliatory, and helpful. In that period, the Americas were a vast land of plenty. The indigenous tribes who lived near what is now called Jamestown did not have a problem sharing the bounty of this land that was provided by the "Creator" for all. They thought it natural and proper. The colonizers, as a result, became comfortable and grateful for their good fortune and the bountifulness of this New World.

In reciprocity for their generosity, Native Americans were grossly taken advantage of by the same people they welcomed and helped settle on their lands. The European behavior toward the indigenous population suggests we were the people who were deceptive, barbaric, deadly, and imaginatively cruel beyond logic or reason. The indiscriminate human slaughter and the things they did to the Native Americans is beyond extreme cruelty or logic. This included not only indiscriminate killings but also mutilating body parts, including those that are private, of Native American men, woman, and children as they killed and plundered toward their goal of land grabbing what is now the whole of the United States. This is very difficult to accept, understand, forgive, or forget. One can easily deduce that although they justified all the above in the name of "God," the European actions were unconditionally driven by greed for land and minerals. Only in recent history has the truth surfaced and the Native American story told with more fairness and accuracy.

Bottom line: If Native Americans became cruel and merciless with animosity toward white folk, it was our odious, pernicious, self-serving behavior that turned them as such. If there is doubt of the accuracy of my observations, supportive evidence is easily accessible and in abundance. Like the Latin phrase often used to prove a point in court, *res ipsa loquitur* (the findings speak for themselves).

An Overview of Communism versus Democracy

Unlike the American Civil War, the Greeks Civil War was fought for the competing ideologies of those times—communism versus democracy. The concept of communism sounds attractive, utopic, egalitarian, and fair. Its principal objective is for all to be equal or have an equal chance at a good, happy, and healthy life. To many, it was about the "haves and have-nots." It sounded very attractive to many. If I lived in the early 1900s up to the mid-1940s, I might have given this political theory serious consideration.

The two world wars and the Great Depression devastated much of the industrial world and took a heavy toll on economics and humanity. This accommodated a rise of dictatorships and communism; however, for now, in my opinion, a utopian lifestyle does not appear viable for many reasons. In application, it has been proven to be a complete and costly failure, especially with regard to human rights and self-determination. Communism in all or most of the world has morphed into brutal dictatorships.

It is my opinion that the key reason for the failure of a utopian lifestyle is that from the primordial period all life forms had to struggle to survive and continue to do so. This translates to competition for survival at all costs. Those who could not compete were left behind or eliminated. The desire to outdo your neighbor and discriminate against those who are not in your immediate family or circle has been nurtured in most, if not all, life forms and has become part of our DNA. I do not see this ending anytime soon. Perhaps humans will one day achieve utopia, and that might be good or bad. But we are still far from that period. When this occurs, we will probably be less competitive, less motivated, less industrious, and less intelligent—at least without the addition of artificial intelligence to our overall human makeup. One can already see the impact to our brains by the technology that make our lives more comfortable. That might be okay and gladly taken, like an addictive drug. But we need to remind ourselves that nothing is for free, and we must find various ways to challenge our minds and bodies if we are to remain human.

Furthermore, although the communist ideology was to commune and live a life that is productive and equal with all, as history clearly demonstrates, it quickly morphed into dictatorships, and equalitarianism was quickly tossed out the window. The cruelty, torture, and elimination of those who opposed this new system is well documented. Magnifying the undesirability of the modern version of communism was Joseph Stalin of Russia. He ruled a brutal dictatorship state with an iron fist and cared not one iota for human rights and equality—only equal and cruel suffering for those who opposed him.

Under Stalin's brutal and oppressive regime, it is estimated that over twenty million Russians and occupied peoples, probably many more, were killed by this madman's paranoia, callousness, and singular adulation for himself. With President Gorbachev's ascendency, there was a year or two of respite and real hope for the long-abused and suffering Russian citizens. With his exit from politics, the ruthless dictatorship came back in the form of Vladimir Putin.

Putin's unprovoked invasion of Ukraine and unbridled cruelty and lies, including launching of hundreds of rockets targeting living areas and schools that killed thousands of old and young people, not military, is nothing short of genocide. All of these because Ukraine wishes to maintain its freedom. As a bully, Putin committed these unspeakable crimes because his military was bested by the Ukrainian soldiers. I think his hero, Stalin, would be so proud of his acolyte! He, too, was a bully with no compassion for humanity or justice.

Before communism, for centuries in Russia there was a wealthy aristocracy who treated the common folks essentially as serfs, just a layer higher than slavery. This monarchy, for the most part of that era, at least in the late nineteenth and early twentieth centuries, was hard on the Russian citizens. My heart bleeds for these peoples. Between serfdom and despotism, life has dealt them a very bad hand that has morphed into an extremely prolonged tyranny. It is time they catch a break so they can begin to live a life worth living, with a promise of a better future.

China is probably a prime example of a communist country that "works," but the principal benefit is strictly economics. All who deviate from the central government directive seemingly pay a heavy price for their counter government comments and actions or their religious beliefs. Case in point, the concentration camps of roughly 1.5 million people—namely, Uyghurs and other Muslims. So much as I respect the

Chinese and their economic success story, I consider them potentially dangerous, with severe repercussions. I would not be surprised if due to lack of resources, such as water, they might start a war that will be disastrous to all. So, when and if the welfare of this world is at stake, the West should continue to work closely with China, but they must watch their backs.

A Brief Overview of Greece's Contribution to World War II

During World War II, surprising to many, the Greeks were the first of the Allies to earn victories over the Axis powers—Germany and Italy. In fact, when the Greeks were beating the Italian war machine back to Italy, Churchill stated, "The Greeks fight like heroes, and heroes fight like Greeks!" Allegedly, the French placed a sign by the Italian side of the Alps that read "Greeks stop here!" Bottom line: the World War II Greeks showed the world that the Axis powers could be beaten.

Greece became involved in World War II when Italy, using Albania as their launching point, decided to invade Greece. Mussolini was getting anxious that he was falling behind Hitler and the highly successful German war machine. He gave the Greeks an ultimatum with a specified time to accept Italian hegemony. Prime Minister Metaxas famously declined on October 28, 1940, with one simple word: "*Oxi* (No)!" Italy then proceeded to invade Greek territory. The Greek army not only stopped the Italian war machine in its tracks but almost immediately pushed them back further and further into Albania, embarrassing Mussolini and necessitating military action from Hitler.

With no victory in sight on the Greek front, Germany was forced to delay their invasion of Russia by five weeks (Operation Barbarossa) and divert twenty-four divisions to Greece to assist their ally to conquer Greece. A similar force was concurrently sent to Yugoslavia. Although Yugoslavia had signed a treaty with Germany, because of Greece's success, there was internal restlessness, and Germany did not wish to be surprised by a successful uprising. This could have significant consequences for Germany. Logistics were a key reason for that invasion. The objective was to protect their supply chains located in Yugoslavia, which were essential to supporting their war effort.

Prior to the surprising Greek victories, the Axis powers in Europe were an unstoppable juggernaut that reaped through Europe and parts of Africa like a well-oiled machine harvesting wheat. It was surprising because the Greek military lacked much in military equipment and supplies necessary to wage war—very few planes, tanks, ships, and submarines, as well as clothing to keep boots on the ground warm in the cold mountainous region that bordered Albania and Greece. Also, its military force was nowhere near the size of the Axis power. At the end of the day, the Greek men and woman truly lived up to their ancestors' heroics of old.

One of those fighting on the Albanian front was George Giannopoulos of Sparta. His feet became gangrened due to lack of proper boots. Their efficacy was compromised by the snow, wetness, and icy cold weather. Before the war, it has been said by his neighbors to his children, that George was an Evzone and served as a guard at the royal palace. The medics wanted to amputate his gangrened toes. The Evzone refused and returned home to Sparta expecting to die. If he was going to die, he reasoned, he wanted to die with all the body parts he came into this world with. This brave soldier got lucky, and his legs eventually healed. In America, on September 26, 1976, George Giannopoulos became my father-in-law. I married his beloved first child, Garifallia! He and his wonderful spouse, Vasiliki, had two additional children: Themistocles and Panagiota.

My father, Gerasimos, concurrently joined and fought in the navy. His ship was torpedoed, and he almost drowned. Both men were patriots who in their own ways made a difference in the war effort. They hardly ever spoke of their involvement in the war. That is what one calls a "hero!" Do your job, do not look for adulation or favor, and move on.

There were many Greek heroes born in this war. One deserves special commendation: Konstatinos Koukidis, a seventeen-year-old on guard duty as an Evzone at the Acropolis. He replaced the Evzone fighting on the Albanian front. It is alleged that the Germans rushed to the Acropolis to raise the Nazi flag. An officer ordered Kostandinos to surrender, give up the Greek flag, and raise the Nazi swastika in its place. Instead, as the story goes, Koukidis took down the Greek flag, refusing to hand it to the Germans, wrapped it around his body, remained loyal to duty and country, and jumped off the Acropolis to his death.

For full disclosure, this story has been recently contested as possibly being war propaganda. This is because local administration recently could not find his name anywhere in the list of Evzones or any other governmental log. Those who disagree with the observation offer two witnesses' accounts: Stathis Arvanitis and Kyriakos Giannopoulos. Both affirm the above to be true. The two witnesses who attested to the accuracy of this event were young when this occurred—Arvanitis, who was seven at the time, testified that he saw the body falling and people screaming. He and his family lived right below the Acropolis. If he is still alive, Arvanitis would be about eighty-six years of age. I assume their testimony was given after the war and probably both were of adult age and of sound mind. Also, there is a marble plaque at the spot where the young Kostandinos fell that memorializes this Evzone's sacrifice for his country.

Koukidis supporters advise that instead of just the German flag, after his brave act, there were two flags flown at the Parthenon—a Greek and a German flag. They state that they do not know of another German-occupied country that flew both flags when occupied. If the two flag comments are verified, it further strengthens the argument that the event is accurate as recorded.

Another point in support is Koukidis's age of seventeen. As early as the mid-1930s, the Greeks, as other nations, emulated the German Youth Movement Program and instituted their own, identical in dress, purpose, and philosophy, but in blue and white colors instead of brown. A main and important difference—Greece did not hate or dislike Jews and did not seek war.

If Koukidis was part of the youth program, it would not be surprising that no record of this young man ever existed. He was dressed as an Evzone because he replaced the Evzone who went to war. That must have been a predetermined role. For this reason, and those previously mentioned, this event is probably accurate as stated. I found the Greek Youth movement information while surfing Google, as well the article on Koukidis's bravery. It was written by Paul Antonopoulos in the Greek news. Finally, Ancestry.com indicates there were Greeks with the surname "Koukidis," at least in the 1900s. All names cited were Greek and those cited lived in Greece; it also suggests the name "Koukides" might be of Yugoslavian origin. This would not be unique. For example, a couple of the many Greek names that suggest foreign origins are

"Arvanitis" suggest Albanian origin and "Voulgaris," Bulgarian. In conclusion, if this was not a true event, why not use a more traditional, well-known name, instead of a unique and uncommon surname with a foreign origin that came to Greece, probably in the late 1800s?

Final Comments on Greece's Contributions during World War II

History suggests—and Hitler and several of his generals agreed—that a key reason Germany lost World War II was Greece's surprising victories against Mussolini and his Italian forces. As previously noted, the victories by Greece caused Germany to halt their entrance to Moscow (Operation Barbarossa) for five weeks and divert twenty-four of their divisions to Greece to help their Italian allies. This included 680,000 soldiers, 1,200 tanks, and 700 aircraft. For logistic reasons, the Germans also sent a similar-sized force to Yugoslavia—this comprised a combined force of 48 divisions, 1,360,000 soldiers, 2,400 tanks, and 1,400 aircraft! Because of the continuous attacks by the local Greek and Serbian freedom fighters, Germany was forced to stay in Greece and Yugoslavia until at least the end of 1943.

The five-week delay allowed the Russians to reinforce and be better prepared for a German invasion. The preparations were inclusive of military equipment provided by the United States, England, and other allies. To further strengthen my argument, despite the five-week delay, the Germans were only ten to twelve miles from Moscow before they were halted due to lack of man, fuel, and military equipment. The taking of this strategic city could have provided shelter from the severe Russian winter, food, fuel, and other resources. The expected easy victory came to an abrupt halt that resulted in a monumental disaster and a total loss at the Russian front. In simple terms, it probably changed the outcome of the war, at least on the European front. Roughly 80 percent of the German soldiers killed in World War II died fighting on the Russian front. Until its decision to halt and divert twenty-four divisions to Greece and Yugoslavia, Germany had sustained minimal losses in all its previous battles.

Some disagreed with Hitler's observation that the delay caused by the Greek victories cost him the war. Those who disagree attribute the

Russian disaster to rising river levels and other factors. Perhaps that was part of it. But I say a resounding bullshit! I say this because Germany was approximately ten to twelve miles from Moscow when they were halted. Would not the twenty-four divisions diverted to Greece with all those soldiers, tanks, planes, and firepower be enough of a difference maker to have allowed the powerful and well-trained German war machine to push into Moscow? If not, why don't we also add the twenty-four German divisions that were sent to occupy Yugoslavia as a direct result of the Greek victories. If the answer is yes, and logic, common sense, and history suggest that it is a resounding yes, I think you will find that the Russian front and World War II in general would have taken a different turn and so would history, especially for the Jewish people and other "enemies" of the German state.

For the record, I do not blame the German people. They were and are good and compassionate people. In fact, I have dear friends in Germany and England who are Germans. But demagogues with ill intent can cause innocent people to become rabid with hate and cruelty, causing them to reconfigure a false narrative of what comprises "humanity." History will tell you that this has happened in the past and will happen again.

In 2020 it almost happened in America. And it is still happening with greater fervor and extremism. 2020 is only the beginning and may be the precursor of worse things to happen to this great nation. Time will tell.

There is so much I would like to say about these sad times in America. But if I start, it will take too long to articulate my disappointment and long-term expectations. Unfortunately, it requires a separate book. And for now, I am too old and too tired. All I will say is I hope this wonderful experiment called America, which had and has so many flaws and so much blood on its hands, in time started to learn from its myriad of errors and became a beacon for the free world and the world in general. As I write this sentence, this magnificent country, with so much promise and potential, is teetering toward chaos and uncertainty with catastrophic "end of days" ramifications. Imagine a small fire in a forest full of dry, highly combustible trees. Once the fire takes hold, it would be almost impossible to stop, destroying everything and anything we humans have built.

For the record, I am just focusing on politics, not the most dangerous variable of all, climate change, which is moving us and Mother Earth, like a juggernaut toward oblivion. I hope the good Lord enlightens the greedy and blind, and helps us realize the danger that this beautiful corner of the universe is in; and with our constructive contributions, the potential to make our Earth, truly, a universal role model and not another Venus or Mercury.

A Special Thank-You to a Special Mentor

A special thank-you to my teacher, principal, and friend—the late Mr. Elias Polites of Socrates Greek American Grammar School. Socrates was tailor-made for the Greek immigrant children of the late 1950s and 1960s. This is the school I attended when I arrived from Greece. The school was housed in a two-story building. It held roughly seventy students and classes only went up to the seventh grade. The original Socrates was much bigger. With migration toward the suburbs, very few Greeks stayed behind, and hence this building and location were selected to service the few who lived close by and those newly arriving immigrants, such as myself.

Mr. Politis's passionate articulation of our history, heroism and the academic contributions by the Greeks to the world, was ingrained deep in my mind and soul. It made me proud to be a Greek. I thought I was Achilles, Theseus, Leonidas, Themistocles, Alexander, Athanasios Diakos, all the above, and more. I thought I was unstoppable and that nothing was impossible. I realize that what I am about to say sounds delusional and weird, and that would be a fair observation and perhaps not far from the truth. That is, I always felt and even now, at seventy plus, that my heroes frequently visit my heart and soul, pushing me onward to do and be the best I can be. For my part, despite my many shortcomings, I try to make them and my family proud. I went to Socrates from the third to seventh grade. For the fourth grade, due to family economics, I went to May School, near Cicero and Congress in Chicago.

In many ways, Mr. Politis was my surrogate father, as my father for many years worked from early morning till late in the day to feed and support his family. Because of his work, I hardly knew the person he was. I got to know him better as I approached adulthood. And once we bonded and talked, we became very close. So close that he would tell his youngest son his concerns and needs. Then I would meet with the brothers to see how we might ease his burden, and we did. More of my father's story will be discussed in his own and my mother's sections.

Our father was the chef at National Cafeteria in the Loop (downtown Chicago). Since then, the building that housed National Cafeteria has been razed to build other more profitable businesses. Looking back, I finally realized my father worked very hard. I wish he were still alive so I could tell him how much I appreciate his many sacrifices and his commitment to family and native country.

FYI, many of the students who went to Socrates, during my time there, had parents who similarly worked long and hard for their families. For immigrant families, that was pretty much the norm.

Mr. Politis liked me, and even in his late years, if he saw family or friends, he would ask them with hopeful anticipation, "Is Ilias here?" A few years ago, I called my friend Gus Tingos to help me organize a celebration for Mr. Politis. I was aware he was old and not in the best of health. I wanted Mr. Politis to know how much we valued and cared for him for his immense contributions as a mentor. And for helping us discover who we were and where we came from. Gus shared we were a year too late. This revelation greatly saddened me. And even though years have passed, it still does.

It is difficult for me to properly articulate the positive impact he had in my young life and probably continues to this day. He cared deeply about his students. Although he never showed it to me, he had a huge temper, if his students did not understand or do well in his small school. I am certain that more than once he slammed with his hand at the chalkboard in trying to educate us. In one of those episodes, he got so upset with Phyllis Giannopoulos, my future wife. Phyllis advised that he hit the board so hard that his knuckles were bleeding. Still, I am confident this minor injury did not stop him from repeating that angry reaction when he felt it was necessary for the academic good of his students. For the record, I have witnessed such an event but they were very rare. I did not witness Phyllis' moment of "truth and consequence," as I had already graduated. Irrespective, his impulsive temper was a sign of how much he cared for his students' educational development.

From my recollection, Mr. Politis was a man of honor and expected his students to be the best they could be. He liked all and cared deeply for all. He explained history to us and the battles the ancient Greeks fought and how or why they won most of the battles fought. Also, mythologies like Persues, Herakles, Thesues, and more and their accomplishments. And every story of mythological heroes or villains he discussed, were intended to be didactic and include a positive moral and educational twist to it. Thus, educating the student in many positive ways-honor, courage, loyalty, commitment, problem-solving and most important, who we are, were we came from and be proud of our origin. That was my friend and mentor, Mr. Elias Politis. Finally, I cannot recall one student who complained about his storytelling. The reason being, I think, is that he took it personal. Clearly, he had a fan and eventually a friend in me. In times of personal battles, whether confronting bullies, academics, or just life's issues in general, I felt empowered. Since Socrates only had seven grade levels, I transferred to Longfellow Grammar School, in Oak Park, for the eighth grade.

As noted, I went to Socrates Greek American School for all but the fourth grade. My first time saying a poem in honor of Greek Independence Day, I said it rapidly and embarrassing. But then I learned to control this weakness. In fact, in a short time, I became the best poet and actor in that school. This was confirmed when Helen Sianis, younger than me by about seven or ten years, and the daughter of John Sianis, a friend of my father's, told her parents that Mr. Politis one day in her class, near retirement with significant age, was reflective of who he thought was the best poet, presenter, and actor of Socrates in his years as principal (roughly twenty-five-plus years). He was speaking to her class and without reservation he said, "Louis Garbis." Truly an honor to be so highly considered by this good man, for whom I had great fealty and respect.

I humbly admit, I became pretty good and was good at improvising. In fact, in one of our annual plays about Greek Independence Day, I had the lead role as a Greek priest who was being stabbed by a Turkish soldier for being a Christian. I asked Mr. Polities if I could improvise; he acquiesced. After being stabbed and falling to the ground, I started shaking my fist at the Turk. As I was lying on the floor dying, with hand clenched into a fist, and both body and hand in a convulsive, spastic rage, with mouth spewing pure hatred, I cursed him and his creed. My friend Gus Tingos, who played the Turkish soldier standing above me with a sword, later told me that he got goose bumps.

May School

For the fourth grade, I went to May School. It was about three blocks from where we lived by Van Buren and Cicero. Early on, I struck a friendship with Denny Pantazis. Denny was in the same grade as I but one year older. His father was no longer alive, nor his mother. He was cared by his older sister and aunt. I felt sorry for him. Denny was a good kid, but not one to defend himself. He would rather walk away if he could or just take the punishment. Unfortunately, he would not defend himself and took the punishment.

At that time, I had not yet sprouted, and I was on the short, stocky side. A Eugene was also in our class. He was very tall with blondish hair and on the thin side. Apparently, Eugene's favorite pastime was to torment Denny at recess. As he was beginning to bully him, I instinctively got in the middle, jumped as high as I could, and punched him in the mouth. The next thing I saw was Eugene on the ground, sitting on his butt with a bleeding mouth with both hands backward, firm on the ground and gazing at the sky. After that, Eugene never bothered anyone. To his credit, Eugene never complained.

Another episode at May School was when all the boys were playing a game pushing and shoving on a team approach. A skinny kid started punching me, so I punched back. The next thing I recall was being called into the principal's office. I was advised that the boy I had hit had fractured ribs, and I was asked if I was going to pay the medical bills. I meant no harm, and I just reacted to a boy my age. Perhaps this poor kid might have been malnourished. I do not recall hitting him that hard. I hope the teachers were just scaring me, and if so, they did.

Return to Socrates

The next year I went back to Socrates for the fifth, sixth, and seventh grades. In the sixth grade, the sixth and seventh graders had a race. From one end of the school yard the other and back. That was roughly a total of two blocks. The school property was all fenced. The fence was probably about eight feet in height.

Phil Geraci was in seventh and considered the top athlete. As his name implies, he was half Greek and half Italian. He had a younger brother named Greg. Their mother was Greek and divorced. When we started running, he was leading all runners, all the way until the final half block. I was about five feet behind him. Then we both turned it on, he quit about twenty feet or so from the end, appeared to be totally spent; I continued and won. When I stopped, my throat had almost closed and wheezing and could hardly breath. I did not panic, and eventually I recovered. That was the first time my throat reacted like this. It would not be the last. On the flip side, rarely, if ever, do I panic. In fact, until retirement, when things got tough or very busy with significant pressure, my mind became more focused, and everything appeared to slow down, allowing me to better handle the situation. As I age, sadly, this important attribute is being eroded.

One day I was outside with a schoolmate, George Kostarelos. We were playing outside the school at end of the north corner of the street. It was winter with some snow and ice on the ground. A tall kid, appeared a year or two older than us, came by and asked me "what are you looking at." I replied in my broken English, in like form, "What are you looking at?" He asked us to stay where we were, and he would be right back with just one more person, implying it would be a fair fight. We waited but not one but probably twenty-plus Italian schoolmates followed him there. It was most likely a gang. All my schoolmates who were outside (no more than seven or eight, as this was a very small school), smartly went inside the fence. Kostarelos did not. In fact, he was holding a good-size piece of ice to use to fight back if needed. I and Kostarelos stayed and waited for Italians to come. To this day I value and appreciate his decision to stay with his friend. George was not a tough guy but he was fearless and loyal.

The tall guy with the big mouth was there but not visible. A stocky kid, my size and probably age named Rocky, was looking at me and one of his friends intentionally pushed him toward me. I reacted and pushed him back. Nothing happened. Then my friend, the late Mike Voulgaris came outside and advised that Mr. Politis asked that I come inside. I looked at Rocky and his friends, and with a sneering demeanor, we went inside.

They were probably embarrassed by their cowardice and felt compelled to erase that episode. As a result, about four or five from the gang came back the next day looking for me. To their bad luck, I had already left to take the train to Oak Park, where I lived. Mike Voulgaris was there with a few kids waiting to be picked up by the assigned car to take them home. They pulled a gun on Mike, made him get on his knees, and beg forgiveness for my actions. The next day I went with Mr. Politis to Pompei School and complained to their principal. We were never bothered again. As a peace offering, we played a softball game against each other. I do not recall who won, which tells me that we lost. After the game, there was no longer any interaction between the two schools.

In the seventh and final grade, my peers and I would roam and discover the neighborhood. One side were the Italians from the School of Pompeii, another side, the Cabrini-Green projects, where poor Blacks and Hispanics lived. I can honestly say the only group who never bothered us were the Blacks. Perhaps that is why I think of them kindly. Case in point, four or five of us boys decided, one day, to enter Cabrini Green and played in their playground. One tall thin Black man with shades came out leaned on the supportive wall and watched us play. He stayed with us until we left. Looking back, I imagined that he was there to protect us from harm; as we meant no harm, but we did not know better either.

Greg Voulgaris, Mike's younger brother, was a good-looking kid. In one of our outside the fence excursions, he saw a Mexican girl and apparently said a few harmless words trying to get her attention. Her brother was the leader of a gang and saw this from a distance. He must have considered this trifle exchange as an attack on family honor and wanted to fight Greg. Greg accepted and the next day we all met in an ally about two blocks from our school-four Greek boys and a similar number of Hispanics. As a side note, it was our general opinion that if Greg had eaten a lot of sugar, he would be more alert and a better fighter. So we stacked him with a lot of sugar and then went to meet the "Mexican" gang. The girl's brother took out a butcher knife and was threatening Greg. I then stepped in and told him to fight like man and use only his fists. A nearby neighbor saw what was developing and called the cops. Oscar, probably a Latin of mixed race and probably second in command of this gang, became nervous that they may get in trouble with the police and took the butcher knife and threw it in the fenced yard next to where we were standing. After that, we all quickly went our separate ways as we heard a police car siren.

After a few weeks had passed on the way to the train station to go home, we encountered Oscar who was with friends. He was either attending or just hanging around a Catholic School that was part of a church. The church was located enroute to the train station. He was trying to bully us. We ignored him and kept on walking. After a few days, Gus Tingos happened to be visiting and was walking with us and a couple of my fellow students toward the same train station. I saw Oscar and friends waiting for us on the opposite side of the street. I assume he wanted to try to bully us again. I shared with Gus what had previously transpired. He asked me if I wanted to confront him. I said yes. Oscar and Gus were about the same size and probably age.

When we walked across the street to confront Oscar and friends, Oscar pulled out a switchblade, about four to six inches in length. Gus told him that if he did not put it away, he would shove it up his ass! Oscar froze. Lucky for Oscar that the priest from the nearby church saw what was going on and came, took the knife, and deprived Oscar from having a sharp, piercing experience of the anal kind!

Gus Tingos was one tough guy. Where I fought *only* when I had to, Gus had no problem looking and finding trouble. He was tall, smart, and loved to debate, which often transpired in assertive arguments among friends, including yours truly. He was and is a good guy and a very close friend. Gus is two years older than me and had finished Socrates before me. But despite the age difference, we were friends through and through, and Gus was a friend to all. More like a big brother. In our old age, we are still friends. Weddings, christenings, funerals of friends, we are usually there. I am comfortable to state, that we will be friends until we leave this earth and probably beyond.

Longfellow Grammar School

Since Socrates only had seven grade levels, I transferred to Longfellow Grammar School, in Oak Park, during the eighth grade. After a couple of months, I was moved from the normal eighth grade to the advanced class. I can assure you it is not because of my natural intelligence but because of my strong work ethic and preparations I had received from Mr. Polites at Socrates.

One friend who I fondly recall from Longfellow Elementary was Mike Gentile. Mike lived about two blocks north from our house on the same street. One day, due to gross stupidity, I almost killed Mike. He came by my house to play. He let me know that he liked to try ouzo. I filled up a regular size water glass to at least three-fourths from the top and I said, "Bottoms up." Trusting me he said, "Cheers," and bottomed it up. As soon as he finished gulping it down, the poor guy started punching his stomach a few times, breathed hard in and out, in and out, then fell to the ground and again went under the faucet and started drinking water as much as he could. He fell to the ground again, still punching his stomach and again, and drank water from the faucet. At some point Mike was able to settle down.

That was very stupid of me and that lesson was learned and never repeated. Thank God Mike was not harmed by my unadulterated stupidity! Youthfulness and foolishness are one coin with different sides. On that day I became that coin. I am grateful and fortunate that Mike had a strong constitution and thankfully was okay.

Oak Park High

At Oak Park High, the first two years I was a very good student. In the second year, I had taken a history class. Because of the number of students, there were two classes taught by our teacher-identical in subject matter. In the other class, he said there was one student who stood out from the rest regarding history—Louis Garbis. Please understand, I did not solicit this comment, nor I am here to brag nor self-adulate; far from that. This was not my intent at all. I just need for my descendants to know a bit of who I was, not what I may become or have become in old age. Also, I would be lying if I did not share with our descendants that my mistakes were many; some, highly disappointing with disastrous results. Hopefully, I learned from my mistakes and became better, more mature and smarter. Unfortunately, it took a while for me to learn from my many mistakes!

For a short period, also in my second year, I joined the sophomore football team. Although I never played contact football, after some intense practices to allow the coaches to determine who plays where, the coach selected me to play first-string middle linebacker (the monster man). Concurrently, Tony needed help at his store, which was located on Central and Lake. With continuing, nonstop family pressure, I acquiesced and quit the team and went after school to work for Tony's grocery store, Central Food Market.

From sophomore year onward, after school I would go home and take a bike that Tony provided me for deliveries. This was an old bike with a metal basket in the front and as a result, a smaller wheel. It was ugly and onerous to ride. I would ride that bike from our house in Oak Park to Lake and Central, about six miles, to where the store was located. I worked from five to nine, then closed the store. After work, I would follow the same path with the bike. This lasted about a year. After that, a car was given to me by Ted, a red Chevrolet Impala. It was a great car and a good ride, until my friends and I slowly but surely, turned this beautiful car into a drivable tin can. A sad ending to a great car! It was generous and brotherly for Ted to give his kid brother this quality automobile for free.

After coming home from the grocery store around ten, I would commence my homework, which often lasted past midnight. Doing math one night, at around two in the morning—either algebra or trigonometry, I do not recall which I was having a difficult time solving a problem. After a while, I got so upset I swore in Greek, "*Gamoto!*" It is kind of like saying, "Damn it," but in a more vile but still harmless way, if this explanation makes sense. As I swore, I pounded my fist on the table so hard that all woke up frantically, inquiring what had happened.

Still upset with my inability to solve this problem, I told them what was going on and angrily asked them to go back to sleep. I could hear my brother Bill saying in disbelief, "Oh … my … God!" Then all awakened went to sleep, followed by me a bit later.

Going back to football, the football team I left behind in my sophomore year won the Suburban League Championship! Having to quit the football team made me bitter for a while, as the move not only eliminated any chance of a sports scholarship but it also affected my academic endeavors. For the reasons stated above that involved after schoolwork, I was always tired, which did not allow me to maximize my efforts to excel in school.

Looking back, however, that was the correct choice, and Tony deserved this assistance and more from his kid brother. Tony and I became very close prior to his passing. He advised me of his young years in Kefalonia and his ongoing hard work and sacrifices to help feed a starving family. This has been noted in the sections referring to

Andoni (Tony). He and Denny sacrificed much and were instrumental to our family's welfare in one of the more critical times in our lives.

So, to help me write our story, after he made me aware of his young life in Kefalonia, there is nothing I would not have done for this brother of mine, who at a very early stage in his life took on gargantuan tasks that made a difference to our family's well-being. Much of his contributions were articulated under his section "Andonis." So I will not repeat that here. I am amazed at his commitment to family and toughness to achieve desired results. My personal sacrifice compared to his is totally irrelevant!

University of Illinois Chicago

Remember: I tend to speak fast. This is in part a family trait, perhaps on the Garbis-Meselouraiko (Grandmother Anastasia's) side. It appears my vocal cords and brain are not firmly connected and when especially excited, I speak fast, or the words do not come out and it would be easier for me to physically act then articulate a point, especially when I am angry and arguing with someone I do not like. Most likely, this impediment would have ceased and the connection between brain and vocal cord solidified, had I not been driven to endeavor to be the best I could be in a dynamic and demanding academic environment.

Case in point, although I have a natural and strong inclination toward history, when I went to the University of Illinois, Chicago Circle Campus, I chose the business school. Right or wrong, I thought it was the best way to get a job after graduation. Since then, my brain never forgave me. For a long period of time, it was fighting me every step of the way. It was telling me, but I chose to ignore it. "Idiot. You were born to be a historian! So, with your betrayal, I will make your life miserable!" Metaphorically speaking, it did. The change from history to business was like leaving a nice, comfortable walk in the park, and deciding to join the French Foreign Legion and endlessly fighting the Arabs on their own turf, on a tower up high, and playing the bugle like the great classic, "Beau Geste!" If that does not kill you, it will wear you down. And it did, and it has.

Despite my brain's strong objections, I did well. For example, in my first year, from a grades standpoint, I was rated to be in the upper ninety fifth percentile of the total U of I student population. But then, for personal reasons, that resulted in disastrous consequences, I became lost and pretty much transformed into an average student. I must have been influenced by the college environment and the times.

In my fourth and final year, I kind of came out of my "funk." I did better and graduated with a BS in business administration. To my surprise, the economics professor who headed the newly created master's in economics department asked me to join him. He wanted me to be his teaching assistant (TA) for the masters of economics class. Being independent minded and naive of potential and possibilities, I thank him but declined. I wanted to join an MBA program, which at that time, U of I, Circle Campus, did not have. Being a TA in the economics master's program would have probably been an easier path toward business success, and most likely I would have become an economist.

Interestingly, I always have chosen the harder paths of life. Often for good reasons. From my vantage point, I wanted to be the best I could be and right or wrong, that was the way I thought I was going to accomplish my personal and professional goals. At the end of the day, despite the heavy mental cost, everything worked out fine. And although I have come far, made a difference to my clients, and have done well for my family, I can only wonder how far and what impact I might have had if I had specialized in history.

Career in Risk Management and Insurance

After completing my academic career and receiving an MBA from Roosevelt University, I was offered and accepted a position in risk management at Abbott Laboratories. Abbot was a global organization that specialized on a worldwide basis in manufacturing drugs and diagnostic equipment for the healthcare industry. It was a tremendous education on the job for me, willingly provided by two great professionals—Earl Zander, director of risk management, and James Nesci, manager of claims. Earl trained me in finance and professional presentations, verbal or written. Jim trained me in claims and litigation. Both were excellent mentors—Jim was especially helpful, as I learned a great deal about law, claims, and negotiations. The skills I acquired in academia and at Abbott were invaluable to my professional development. This included but not limited to negotiations, analytics and problem-solving, especially as an Account Executive servicing large, global corporation in respect to their insurance and risk management needs. After a year I was made supervisor, handling on a nationwide basis all claims-either direct adjustment or claims in litigation. This required working with some of the best lawyers that money could buy. It was rewarding, educational and fulfilling.

After leaving Abbott, I found my way to a national broker, Frank B. Hall. Early on in my new career as an insurance broker, it was obvious that to succeed with large national firms in this highly competitive field, you must win and win much more than lose. As a result of this revelation, I would always remind myself that "second place is last place." I would say this to myself, and any other associate who was willing to listen. This awareness made me more attentive, focused, and aware of my precarious surroundings. As a result, throughout my career, I worked nonstop to continued upgrading my skills and proficiency in my chosen field; and it benefitted me and my family greatly. Because of solid foundation I obtained in risk management and Insurance, as well as by my MBA, in time, I could tangle with almost any person or company irrespective of size, and from a professional standpoint, whether in marketing, analytics or servicing, they would know they were in for a good fight. More often than not, I would be the victor. I became an effective problem-solver. In hard insurance cycles, when most insurers would decline difficult high-risk programs, I was one of the few that more than not, was able to effectively articulate to underwriters why they should provide terms of coverage. Often they acquiesced. That was especially demonstrated in the mid-1980s, when the casualty market became very tight. Securing general liability (GL) occurrence coverage was almost nonexistent—except for a very few, including yours truly. In that era, for about four years, the only coverage provided by insurers for GL was underwritten on a claims-made basis—an inferior coverage for most GL exposures and, if possible, should be avoided. As the insurance market returned to normal, this problem became a nonissue.

Even now, I always look for education of any type. The sad part is that with my age advancing, the memory is eroding and sometimes "you learn something more than once." Nevertheless, since it feels like the first time, as sad as it may sound, it still feels okay.

General Observations of Greeks in Foreign Lands

Because history is so strongly embedded in the Greek psych, I doubt that those that were born in Greece ever forget the love of their place of origin; even though they left their homeland for a better life. I assume we minimize or forget why we left and embellish it with nostalgia of prior, imagined times. Of interest are the descendants of those who came to America. They oftentimes follow and revere the traditions of their ancestor's homeland more fervently than their immigrant forebearers. Not surprising, when you love and miss those who preceded you, you venerate and honor their memory and follow the traditions they taught you. I saw this at our church at Saint Athanasios and pretty much any Greek church that I have attended or visited.

Many second- and third-generation Greeks ardently follow the traditions and customs of their parents, whether it be roasting lamb on a spit, Greek dancing, faithfully attending church, and more. Also, I have seen numerous non-Greeks who marry Greeks and enthusiastically follow these same traditions, even more than the Greeks! Yours truly included among those apathetic Greeks. On the other hand, my sister-in-law Susan is one of those prime examples. Susan is of Northern European and Native American lineage. She learned to cook Greek like a Kefalonian and speaks better Greek than me! She truly has embraced the Hellenic heritage. No doubt, the love for my late brother Bill and feeling loved and accepted by all motivated her to integrate and blend into our family. And our family has been much enriched by her inclusion. She is kind, sincere, honest, liked and respected by all. She says what she means and means what she says. Susan has what is called in America "true grit!"

In conclusion, until my late twenties, I was one of those who did not think much about my origins. I was, I suppose, apathetic and focused on my ephemeral needs and working hard to succeed in my profession. With age, marriage, and children, that changed. I guess all three woke me up!

CHAPTER 5

The 1996 Brotherly Excursion to Kefalonia

A Man of Honor

In my forties, I began recalling that when I was about three or four years old, a young shepherd boy of about seventeen befriended me. He would come by the house daily with his sheep and goats that were grazing nearby. He would milk one of the animals and provide me with its milk. To this day, I can see that little boy with a crew cut, holding a small cooking pan with both hands and slowly drinking this vital nourishment; slowly, one gulp at a time. And the shepherd boy, standing next to me, as I drank the milk, patiently looking at me with compassion. I recollect that he was tall and fit, and wearing a whitish sheep skin jacket. But who was this good Samaritan? Much as I tried, I could not recall who he was and that frustrated me.

Since we did not have any livestock, let alone ones that produced milk, and could not afford to buy any, as a substitute, my mom would give me a small glass of retsina wine with my meal. I would sit outside on a rectangular table of normal size and eat whatever mom could muster up for the day and drink Retsina. I remember those moments fondly.

In 1996 my brothers Tony, Bill, and I went together to Kefalonia. At the village *kafenio* (coffee shop) we met many of our friends and neighbors. They were older than me, and I did not recall anyone. Then one of them asked if I remembered anything from my youth. Not much I responded, but that recently I had a reoccurring memory of a kind young shepherd boy who befriended me by giving me milk from his flock. I also shared it frustrated me because I could not recall who that was. The person who asked the question, I later found out, was George Mihalatos, a friend of the family. He was in his mid- to late fifties.

George then responded that he was that shepherd boy. Astonished by this revelation, I hugged George as if he was a long-lost brother. I thanked him and begged him to allow me to express my gratitude and reciprocate the generosity he had shown me; anything he wanted I would have gladly given him. His kind act meant a great deal to me. George's reply was laconic and to the point—he lacked nothing of importance and thanked me for my generous gesture. He ended by advising that it was enough that I was well. How can you verbally respond with clarity after such a noble comment? Georgios Mihalatos was a rare breed indeed. He was a friend of the family, and most importantly, a man of honor. In my later years, I often think of this good man's goodwill and still become sentimental. When I was younger, tears and emotions were not in my vocabulary. That was a long time ago.

I planned to return the following year and surprise George with a hunting gun, clothes, and whatever else I could find of value for this quality person. Sadly, I learned he had passed prior to my planned travels. It was cancer. I wonder if the Chernobyl disaster of 1986 that permeated much of Europe with radiation also contaminated this man as well as my brother Tony.

A Night to Remember—or Not!

That first night in Kefalonia was momentous, at least for me, but not in a good way. Kefalonians not only love to sing, but many have voices to back it up. Some can make it a successful career. Although I love to sing, yours truly is not one that would have an iota's chance of making it. Even as a "village" singer, let alone professionally! That evening, all my brothers' friends congregated at the *kafenio* (local coffee shop) to meet up with us. I wish I could name them. Bill and Tony, who could, have passed. Besides George Mihalatos who provided me with milk as a child, I can name two from about seven who were there with us that were visiting from America-Nick Garbis aka "tsipourini" a class act in his early fifties and a fun and good guy. We were not relatives, at least not in the modern era, but we called each other "cousin." He was at least Tony's age or about twelve years older than me. That nickname was given to Nick because as a boy, he fell into a barrel that was filled with *tsipouro*—very similar to the American moonshine. Nick would look at me as an older brother with affection and say, "There is something special about you, Ilia." I wish he were right. I do not feel special. Just one who endeavors to be a good person and a good man and on occasion surprises himself and does good.

The other was Montazatos. A Kefalonian that could sing well but not as good as the locals. He was good-looking and, in his fifties, had a likable personality. Montazatos owned a banquet hall in the Chicagoland area and was well known. They were all friends of Tony, Bill and Ted. When they started to sing, not only were the songs beautiful but these guys could really sing!

We were at Cleo's coffee shop. Cleo was tall, thin, kind and a good friend of the family. Her shop was about a block upstream from our family home. She must have been in her mid-fifties. Cleo would serve us ouzo but not in the typical small ouzo glass. The ouzo was served in a glass with a circumference at the top as that of a normal-sized ouzo glass but at least twice its height!

At some point came an old man with a guitar and a tuner. He would go "Eeee," trying to match his voice to the sound of his tuner, and then try to match the sound with his guitar until he got it right. "Eeee" was tried several times. So much that some of us, partly intoxicated, would join him when he practiced "Eeee" and laughed like goofballs. I do not know this older gentleman's name, but I did learn his nickname, "*O ios Tou Amarantou* (the Son of the Immortal)." It is alleged he was awarded this title when he was much younger and became so upset with his father that he attempted to kill him by pumping carbon monoxide from his car with a tube through a window where his father slept. His dad did not die and acquired the nickname of "the Immortal!" Hence his son was elevated to "the Son of the Immortal." The real Kefalonians, as a rule, are witty and enjoy playful banter. Kefalonians are also creative in giving each other nicknames. In the modern Greek language, "immortal" is called *Athanatos*. *Amarandos* must be an older, ancient version of Greek. It is derived from the amaranth plant. It literally means "unfading." Leave it to the Kefalonians to create their own version for describing immortality!

After the Son of the Immortal got comfortable, a beautiful chorus of singers started singing oldie but goodie serenades. Although my voice was not made for singing, I started to sing along; I could not help myself; admittedly, I love to sing, especially when I shower and the running water and the echo generously embellishes the sound of my voice. On that special evening, funny as it may sound, the more ouzo I drank, the more assured I became that my voice was *really* good! Like they say in Greek, *Kano'ni* (cannon). After three or four ouza, the Son of the Immortal played a song that really touched my soul, and those who know me well know I am a very soulful person! We all started singing. It was a love song and a beautiful serenade. Below are the words translated into English:

> Verses: "On one of those sunsets, like a dream, like a spring day, on one of these sunsets, I await you.
> You will come one night with a red rose, you will come one night, I await you."

And then the tenors and rest of us who comprised the chorus joined in with the below refrain.

> Refrain: "Life is short. Come, my love, and leave in the morning; life is short, like a rose that slowly blossoms, then quickly withers away!"

This translation does *not* do justice to the power and beauty of this love song when it is sung in Greek, especially by great singers. It's beautiful and tender phraseology touched my soul as if struck by lightning. I became a different "Lou," resulting in me drinking in short order at least three or four more of those double-sized ouzos, one after the other, one after the other...

My brother Bill, dressed in shorts and a sleeveless gray sport-type T-Shirt, was leaning on a roughly four-foot wall that was protecting him from the ledge. He was about three feet from where I was seating and was curiously studying me, half smiling and a bit confused at the behavior from his kid brother. Like trying to tell me, "Have you completely lost your mind? What happened?" Bill had never seen this part of me. To tell the truth, neither had I.

I looked at him, smiled, and mumbled with a touch of slur, in English, "Brother, you will have to carry me home."

Partly laughing and partly serious, he answered, "Not me! You are too dam big."

And he was right. At that time, I was probably about 290-plus pounds, and the excess weight was not muscle.

I then got up from my chair and went by the side of the wall, where Bill was leaning backward for support. I hunched over the wall and threw up about a couple of spoonfuls of ouzo. As I sat down, both the left and right sides of the top of my forehead felt as if they were lit with gunpowder on two thin lines, moving with lightning speed from the front to the back of my head as if it was a wildfire. This sensation started quickly and ended quickly.

Nick Garbis (tsipourini) had a Jeep. He and Bill—maybe more—pushed me up on the passenger side of the Jeep and drove me to Tony's house, where the three brothers were staying. Bill and Tony had rooms on the first floor. My bed was in the basement. I drunkenly took my clothes off and went to lie down and sleep.

As soon as I laid down, I quickly jumped up and started running in my underwear toward the bathroom, approximately twenty-five feet from the bedroom. I did not quite make it. I'm not sure how much I was able to throw up in the bathroom bowl, but I am certain it was not much. My poor sister-in-law, Tony's wife, Antoinette, was very kind. She cleaned all that mess from the floor and never spoke of it. Thank God the floor was all marble! Knowing Tony's pecuniary proclivities, he would have made me pay for a brand-new floor!

The next day, when I opened my eyes, as it was the basement and very dark and quiet, for a few moments I was not certain if I was alive or dead. I felt comatose. It was very quiet and dark in the room with all shudders shut. Eventually I got a hold of myself and got up. The whole basement smelled like a distillery that specialized in producing ouzo. I am confident my older brother Tony and spouse were not pleased with this development. If so, I totally agree and apologize to all.

Didactically, Bill, and I am certain especially Tony, wanted me to pay a price for my overindulgence, and I surely did! Accordingly, I, with a headache, with the brothers walked downhill from Tony's house to the shore of Trapezaki, all the way the shore of our neighboring village, Lourdata and then up a steep winding asphalt road (50 percent incline) that took us back to Tony's house. All in all, about three-plus miles. But the heat, the difficult-to-navigate rocky shoreline, and the steep, inclined road wrapped around last night's indulgence was not a good recipe for this walk. Still, praise be to God, I survived.

One neighbor asked Bill, "Does Ilias always drink like this?" Bill shrugged as if saying, you know as much as I do. As a rule, I very rarely drink, and when I do, it is insignificant. But I found out on that fateful night, in front of my fellow Kefalonians, that if the music touches my soul, drinking is like an addiction. This does not portend well for future, similar gatherings.

CHAPTER 6

Relatives

Gerasimos (Father)

From my vantage point, my father was a good, fair, and honorable man. The one apparent weakness, if pushed far enough, he could develop a very bad and dangerous temper. Recall the incident previously cited involving my brother Ted. Once he lost it, it appears it was difficult for him to calm down. Personally, I have never witnessed that side of my father. But I am certain it manifested itself on occasion before I was born or old enough to remember.

Based on what little I know of his involvement in World War II and the Greek Civil War, he was a guy you did not want to mess with. He was a patriot who fought for his country and his beliefs. As most veterans of that era, he did not speak much of his involvement in World War II or the Civil War. What I do know was passed down to me by my older siblings and mother. The only information my father shared with me was the sinking of the ship he served on.

My father joined the Greek Royal Navy at the start of World War II. The ship he served on was torpedoed, and he barely made it to shore. He was exhausted from the ordeal. When he reached land, a fellow sailor who was on shore helped him out of the water. I do not recall the name of the vessel. This is all I know of his experience in World War II.

World War II, the Greek Civil War, and the accompanying famine tested many people's temper, patience, behavior, and character, especially when there were many mouths to feed and solutions limited or nonexistent. In those difficult times, I understand that my father and mother would argue loudly and not too irregularly. Sadly, that was probably the norm not the exception for those that were financially destitute and mentally and physically spent.

As much as they argued, my father never hit my mother. But there were others that did. One fellow villager had a kind and beautiful wife. Apparently, his method for decompressing in those very difficult times, on occasion, if he had a tough day, and with minor instigation, was to take a tree branch and whip his wife's legs while she was walking back from the fields. So sad for her and others like her.

Only a small person would revert to such hideous and public humiliations and torture! From what I have heard, this man was not a bad person, most likely, just a sad manifestation of the times. He must have been miserable and took out his frustrations on his poor wife. Nevertheless, for real men, that is never an excuse. Beating or bullying another person, especially a woman, even an animal, just because you can, is inexcusable!

Our father partook in a brutal and bloody civil war that pitted families against each other. He was targeted to be assassinated at least twice. He must have been active, valuable and an effective asset. He was targeted and caught by the Frangata Communist faction—his village of birth. My father was in process of being hanged by being dropped in a dry well near the Saint Gerasimos Church/monastery.

One of its leaders, from a short distance away, realized what was happening and quickly stopped it. He said, "This is a man with a family and six children. If anyone touches him, he will have to answer to me!"

Our father was saved by Gerasimos Maravegias; A family friend and a leader of the Communist faction in Frangata. In my later years, when I learned of Maravegias's defense of my father. I asked around to find and meet him and personally thank him. Unfortunately, Gerasimos Maravegias had passed. In my next trip to Greece, I shall endeavor to find where he is buried in Frangata and place flowers on his grave. We, the descendants of Gerasimos and Arsinoe, must never forget this good man's gift of life to our father and family.

The body of Saint Gerasimos is at the monastery and although he died in August 15, 1579, his body has never decomposed. He is venerated and highly regarded by the faithful. He is visited by many ethnicities from all over the world on a regular basis.

Another story advised to me by my brother Denny, occurred on a stormy day at our home in Vlahata. This was originally the home of the late Panagiotis Markadonatos, Denny's and Dina's father. Denny heard noise and footsteps coming toward the house and warned our father. Our father then took his rifle and went up and perched in a tree close by the house with his rifle pointed at the intruders as the heavy downpour continued. I'm not certain the number of Communists, but eventually my mother convinced them that he was not home, and they left.

As a matter of background, the Communists wanted Greece to mirror Yugoslavia. A good amount of Greek Communist sorties grew from there. After attacking preselected targets, the insurrectionists would return to Yugoslavia to avoid capture. The Democratic faction wanted Greece to remain with the West. The Left wanted to follow Yugoslavia and become communist. In that period, Yugoslavia was probably a proxy of and influenced by Russia.

Russia was "seemingly" passive due to its agreement with England to not interfere. This is when Churchill, unbeknown to Roosevelt, who at that time was very sick and near death, flew to Russia to negotiate and divide much of Eastern Europe with one of the biggest murderers of all time, Stalin. In his negotiations, Churchill insisted that Greece stay under British influence. More importantly, thanks to the Marshall Plan that soon followed and support from the United States, Stalin's objective was never realized. I say this not due to verifiable proof but because of Stalin's well-known fox-like and successful tactics with the West. I am confident Stalin would not have minded turning Greece into a communist state. The West and East both coveted Greece due to its strategic location, which included access to the Suez Canal, which in turn allowed easy access to the Asian countries, such as India and other territories under the English Commonwealth.

History indicates Stalin was cunning and played a lot of deceptive games with Roosevelt and Churchill. Case in point, at the Yalta Conference, where the three superpowers were to decide the future of Europe, Stalin covertly installed microphones in their rooms where they would meet to discuss how to cope with Russia postwar and other important issues of that era. Stalin would listen to what was said and then meet with them and discuss the topic of the day. These tricks and deceptions served him well at the expense of the Allies and half of Europe, which the Allies allowed him to invade and control. How sad and how stupid for two intelligent and seasoned nations to allow a deviant who would have been destroyed by the Germans, if not for their immense support in weaponry, to allow him to enslave, torture, and kill citizens of prewar, free nations!

It is a matter of record that the Greek Communist, even before World War II ended, were aggressive in killing the opposition they considered a threat to their objectives. It is safe to state that American financial assistance via the Marshall Plan and English strategic recommendations to the Greek freedom fighters were vital to winning the Civil War.

A Father-and-Son Spiritual Moment

When I was in my teens, my father and I hardly ever talked. We were like day and night. When I became married and more mature, he and I became very close. So close that on one early Sunday morning I felt uncomfortable and shared with Phyllis that I thought something was wrong with my father. I then called him, and he said, "My son, I am in pain." I asked him to describe what he felt and where. What he described were clear signs of a heart attack. I knew this because I was working at Abbott Labs and was heavily involved in medical claims. Phyllis and I drove as fast as we could from Wheeling to Lawrence and Western and took him to the hospital. Although I saved my father's life, by not calling the ambulance right away it probably caused him to lose part of a function of his heart.

About five years later, I dreamt that I was in a huge shopping mall. I was on the first floor, and he was on the second. There was an escalator near my father and people everywhere. When I saw my dad, I kept shouting, "Dad! Dad! Dad!" I could not understand why my father could not hear me. As he turned to directly face me, he did not look at me but looked straight ahead. I saw both of his eyes severely swollen and a dark reddish in color. Concurrently, at about 5:00 a.m., the phone rang, which woke me. It was from Kefalonia. I do not recall who called, but I was advised that my father had just died. Not surprising, there may be a spiritual connection between those you love and those who love you, even if they have passed! And that is a good thing.

Arsinoe (Mother)

Our mother was a wonderful mother and person who was totally committed to her children and family. She was loyal to the core and worked hard for her family. She had many friends in America and in our village. I remember that she enjoyed April Fools' Day and would play pranks on her friends and laugh enthusiastically and enjoy the result. I remember her taking me down to our beach by Trapezaki when I was very small to play by the beach and swim. Until I became a good swimmer, my mother would tie on my back a floating device comprised of two huge dried-out zucchini or pumpkins, or similar, to enable me to stay afloat. They were corked and sealed so the air would not escape. The inside of this product was extracted to allow floatation. My recollection tells me that both were beneficial to help one learn how to swim. But I am not certain which of the two was used or preferred.

Prior to departing from America, while waiting in Athens for the date of departure to America, my mother took me to the Acropolis and the museum that was located within the premises. She must have wanted me to remember a piece of the greatness of this ancient and vibrant country.

In America, our mother had the misfortune of becoming diabetic. As I lived with my parents until I was married, I would inject the insulin into her leg. In her late fifties, she was also diagnosed with glaucoma and cataracts in both eyes. Doctor Panton, who performed the cataract surgery, had neglected to ask if she was diabetic. This was an important question, because if she had the normal approach to removing the cataracts, it would have been modified to account for the glaucoma. By not asking this important question, the result was that our mother became essentially blind from then on until she died. In short, after this surgery, our mother was never the same. She would sit in a chair, feeling very alone, useless, and defenseless. Her energetic, vibrant personality gone to never return. As a result, our mother slowly but surely continued to decline.

After the surgery, she could not function or regain her industrious qualities. At the end of day, the procedure was malpractice. In fact, it is not unfair to state that this malpractice caused her death. As noted under the "Denny" section, our mother tripped down the stairs that she mistook for the bathroom and broke her neck. Blindness clearly played a big role in her demise. She died at the hospital soon after. A sad ending for a wonderful, vibrant person. She would give the "shirt of her back" to those in need. Being new from the old country and ignorant of the American legal system, this doctor dodged a bullet.

Our mother was kind, considerate, dedicated, and caring. Not a mean bone in her body. She was a staunch and unyielding defender for those that she loved, especially her children. Because of the loss of his father, it is fair to say that although she loved all, Denny was her weakness, and rightfully so. I cannot remember a time she was not giving it her all for her family. All the love, all the tangible things she had she gladly gave them to us. Like her mother, in the postwar era, she sold whatever she owned that could be sold, so we would not go hungry. She would often pray to God to inflict her with any malaise that her children may be exposed to instead of her kids. In my old age, I often find myself making a similar prayer for my loved ones.

By the way, my mother's name is rare in all of Greece, but more so in Kefalonia. I finally looked it up a few years ago. Arsinoe is a Macedonian name that became famous when Ptolemy took over Egypt. As a matter of background, after Alexander the Great's untimely death, his top generals divided his conquests between themselves. Ptolemy received Egypt and became its pharaoh. Queen Arsinoe was a descendant of his. There were more than one Queen Arsinoe—probably five. Apparently, my mother's godfather, whose name we do not know, was an educated person. He wanted to give her a unique, regal name, and that he did! But I am not certain if we, her descendants, should posthumously thank him or burn him in effigy.

Because in my younger years I did not find her name agreeable, I named my only daughter Katherine, after my sister. Katherine is wonderful name that means "pure" in Greek. Arsinoe is unique, and in the long run it grows on you. If I knew better, I would have followed tradition and named our daughter Arsinoe. Our mother more than earned that honor. I truly regret I did not do so. Thankfully, via my brothers, we have three Arsinoes in the family.

Family Attributes

I feel blessed to born in the family of Gerasimos and Arsinoe Garbis. Despite the many hardships encountered, they were wonderful and loving parents; all they had, whether love, food, etc., they gave unconditionally to their children. They were humble, proud, generous, understanding and forgiving. These are the attributes that all of us should aspire to.

They treated all races with respect and equal. An example of this is when I was in college and a bit on the wild side and single. My mother begged me to find a nice girl and get married. I mischievously responded, "And if she is Black?"

My mother replied, "*Pedi mou* (my child), all I care about is for your happiness. If you are happy, I am happy." What else can I say about my mother that is not clearly articulated by her response?

As most parents, our parents were the foundation for their children's behavior and conduct. Judging from my siblings, they did a good job. We are honest, did not and do not do drugs, brag, or similar BS, steal, or live lives of ill repute. Not in our DNA. All have been excellent parents and providers to their families.

Another important family "compass of life" was bestowed upon us by our grandfather Nikolas Garbis. His life suggest humility, pride, honesty and doing the right thing-even if it killed him. He was a poor man, probably of normal in height and a peaceful person. He comes across as agreeable, kind, and a loving family man who never looked for trouble.

From my mother and her side, we inherited boldness, a desire to excel, and toughness. Also, for the lucky few, good singing voices. Our uncle Vasilios, my brother Denny, our uncle Father Dionisios Kourouklis, and cousin Father Ioannis Mesolouras had and have excellent singing voices. In my opinion, the best among the four clearly is Father Ioannis, then Uncle Vasilios, then Father Dionisios, and then Denny.

From my father's side, the Pavlatae were also no pushovers. They were smart, generous, industrious, and bold. They were the ones from our clan who came first to America. Andreas, the oldest, came in the early 1900s and then brought his younger brothers—Athanasios and Gerasimos. They probably also gifted us with height. Ted shared that our grandma, Ekaterini, Nikola's wife, had blond hair. As a young boy, I remember her being on the tall side, as was her first child, my aunt Eleni. In fact, three of Eleni's sons were also on the tall side. Gerasimos, Michalis, and Dionisios, in that order, with Gerasimos being the tallest. The shortest, with a lot of personality, is Nikolaos. He took his height and from his father Spiro, who was a good and highly likeable human being. Maria, the youngest, is also of good height.

Although all my parents' children were tough enough, none looked for trouble, never joined gangs, did drugs, or acted as troublemakers.

But we did not shy away from bullies, especially those who bullied the meek, weak, and women. That became instinctively inherited—probably from the Kouroukli side.

My uncle Vasilios was an example of this trait. Although short, he was tall in stature and boldness. When he returned to his village after World War I, he defended my grandfather Nikolas from three brothers who were bullying him. Their family's nickname was *Malliandonaeee*. This loosely is interpreted as "the clan of Anthony who are hairy." I did not know of the defense by my uncle of my grandfather, until I became an adult. That was admirable and noble of him.

I, too, have more than once went to the defense and rescue of those that could not defend themselves against bullies. This characteristic must be part of our DNA and if so, that is good. Unfortunately, Vasilios had another trait that was not complementary. It will be discussed in the pages that follow under "Vasilios Kourouklis."

Athanasios and Reggina

When I visited my aunts Antelini and Mimoula, I saw a picture of Athanasios, the third son, that included my uncle Spiro. Both handsome young men. Thanasi had learned how to play the violin. Not sure how proficient he was. A picture of a young Thanasi holding the violin is included in the appendix. The picture I saw at the family home suggested he was about five years older than the photo in the appendix and handsome, as was my uncle Spiro. Unfortunately, that picture is lost.

Thanasi was in love with one of the daughters of Tahidromo, the village mailman. By all accounts, she was a beauty. Her name was Reggina with a hard *g*. Tahidromos was also a family friend. Thanasi had a physical condition, which albeit not debilitating, was noticeable. He was bowlegged. One day, as he and Reggina met by a favorite tree, his shotgun went off, resulting in the death of the girl he loved. To the best of my knowledge, no one alive knows the truth. I am aware of two possibilities of what may have transpired. Either the girl made fun of his bow leggedness and threatened to not marry him, an argument ensued, and Thanasi lost control of his "Garbis" temper and shot and killed his true love. Or, in the heat of passion, or just being playful, the gun accidentally discharged, and his beloved Reggina lay on the ground dead. Irrespective of which of the possibilities is accurate, this beautiful and much-loved girl was dead.

Thanasi panicked and ran. Either by rumor or deduction, the police concluded it must have been the father who killed the daughter in anger due to her indiscretions with Thanasi. The father was jailed. These kinds of events were rare but not unique. A similar story was told in the 1950s when a brother killed his sister because she refused to stop seeing a man who the family did not approve of. The brother then dismembered her body and threw it in a well. This "honor" killing occurred somewhere else; not in Kefalonia. Also, Greeks in general are more civilized and humane in respect to such clandestine, amorous affairs. They are not extreme nor unsympathetic to love. They usually acquiesce to their child's wishes. This killing by the brother of the sister was an aberration of reality.

After the arrest of Reggina's father, Thanasis told my grandfather Nikolaos what transpired. With what must have been unimaginable pain because our grandfather loved his son and could envision how this story would end, responded "*Yiee mou* (my son), you already have killed our friend's daughter. Do you aim to also kill her father, the breadwinner, and hence ruin his family too?" He urged his son to go to the authorities, although he recognized that doing so was tantamount to sentencing his son to death. Heeding his father, Thanasi turned himself in, accompanied by his father.

While incarcerated, he gave his bed to a sick cellmate. Sleeping on the floor, he contracted consumption (tuberculosis). Especially in that era, it was a deadly and highly contagious disease. As a result, after a few months, Thanasi was released.

Thanasi went by his mother's house to say his goodbyes. Fearing contamination of her and the rest of the family, my grandmother refused to let him into the house and requested that he immediately leave. I assume our grandmother was also not pleased with Reggina's death at his hands. She knew her well and I am certain that she was very upset at the death of this good neighbor by the hand of her son!

Dejected, Athanasios said his goodbyes to his mother for the last time and left. He then walked about fifteen miles to Vlahata, where my father lived with my mother and at that time their five children. Bill and I were not yet born. Our father gave his younger brother food to eat and put him up in a room for the night. After Thanasis' long walk to

Vlahata and wasted by consumption, he must have been near the end of his young life, and he knew it. The next day our father gave his younger brother as much food as he could and bid him goodbye. This must have been a heart-wrenching goodbye for both. Then Athanasios left, never to be heard or seeing again.

As soon as Athanasios departed, our father took all the blankets and clothing he touched and slept on and burned them. It was the smart thing to do and our father was an intelligent and considerate brother. This is only one example of our father's common sense, humanity, and class.

Athanasios death is registered in the local government records as July 6, 1944. He was twenty-six years old. No one alive knows where he passed or where he is buried.

Later in life and in America, I met the deceased girl's eldest brother, who was good friends with my father. His name was also Gerasimos. He was the son-in-law of Mrs. Mihelou. She owned a successful Greek oriented grocery store by Central Avenue and Harrison Street. The store was juxtaposed the Greek church, Panagia (Virgin Mary). Her son-in-law Gerasimos was the manager of the store.

A few years later, I also met two more of Reggina's siblings when they migrated to America. Even after all these years, when they met me for the first time, a relative of Thanasis, one could still see the pain in their eyes from that sad and senseless tragedy. Perhaps I reminded them of Thanasi, who was about the same age as me when their sister was killed. More poignant, one could see from Reggina's sisters and nieces how beautiful this girl must have been. It is an axiom of life that one split second can bring you immense happiness or total disaster, depending how the dice rolls? Sadly, the dice rolled the wrong way for poor Reggina and Thanasi. It still makes me sad at this unfortunate and disastrous ending of both, especially Reggina the beautiful.

Respect and Honor the Ancestors

In 2012 Phyllis, my family, and I visited our parents' village of Frangata. I asked our late uncle, Father Dionisios and Protopresbyter of the church in Frangata if he could show me the family plot of our grandfather Nikolaos. He took me to the cemetery in Frangata and pointed to a completely unfinished plot. It looked more like an area where animals may rest or hang out or do their business. It was totally neglected and beyond embarrassment for the descendants of Nikolaos and Ekaterini! It did indicate the rectangular design of the plot but no stone to cover and embellish the grave would have included our ancestors buried there. That would include our grandparents and all their children, except Dionisios, who died in Panama, and Thanasi who died from consumption, and whose body was never found; Spiro, who died in America; Gerasimos, our father, who was visiting and died in Vlahata and was buried there; and the youngest, George, who died much later in Frangata and had his own plot prepared for his death.

When I saw this so called "grave," my jaw clenched, I took a deep breath, slowly and rhythmically, body tensed in disbelief of this surreal visual, and my mind was racing at warp speed with negative feelings. I became very sad, fell silent, but my face said everything. I was very hurt and upset at seeing the decrepit condition of the grave site, which to me was a holy site for the purpose of honoring and remembering our ancestors.

I implored my uncle to please, as soon as possible, order the best stone and plot arrangement covering available. Cost was not to be a consideration. I wanted my ancestors to rest in a grave that was reflective and worthy of who they were; and to thank them for their vital contributions for who we have become-good people, good citizens and to date, financially sound.

My uncle, seeing the change in me, gently assured me that he will get a very fine covering and it will be reasonably priced. He more than kept his word. The grave is now decorated with beautiful stones and worthy of our ancestors. For that, I am forever grateful. It also lists all who are buried there as well as one who is not-Athanasios whose body was never found. Those buried there are Nikolas, Ekaterini and all their children that died in Frangata except their Youngest, George. As previously noted, He has his own plot. Thank you, Uncle and Reverend Father Dionisios! May your memory be eternal and may the good Lord continue to bless your family. Now when I visit Frangata, the first stop I make is always to our ancestor's grave.

My uncle kept insisting that this upgrade of the family grave should be engraved and acknowledged as a gift from the grandson, Ilias Garbis. I thanked him but insisted that it not be as he suggested. After a few back-and-forths, he accepted my reasoning. I asked that it only show that it was bequeath by the descendants of the family of Gerasimos and Arsinoe Garbis. He complied with my instructions.

In hindsight, if I were not so extremely angered by what I saw, I would have made a more lucid, proper decision regarding the dedication. I would have considered the local environment and how it shapes and sometimes blinds all of us who are born and raised there, in not seeing the obvious and accepting things as you find them. I should not have forgotten that I have deep feelings and respect for most of my relatives who I consider close friends, family and fine people. The plaque should have been engraved as bequeathed by "the descendants of Nikolaos and Ekaterini Garbis." For that oversight, I ask my cousins and relatives for their forgiveness.

Anastasia (Tasia) Kourouklis

Our mother, Arsinoe was the third child of Panagiotis and Anastasia Kourouklis (maiden name Mesolouras). Panagiotis and Anastasia also had Christopher, the firstborn and Basilios, the second born. I do not know much about my maternal grandfather, Panagioti. It is my understanding that he died in his late twenties or early thirties in early 1900s. His passing was around the era of polio, tuberculosis, and the Spanish influenza. Any one of those could have been sufficient to cause my grandfather's demise. It is estimated that more than fifty million people, globally, lost their lives due to the Spanish flu. From what little I know, Panagiotis Kourouklis was a good and honorable man. With her spouse's passing, our grandmother had to raise the three children on her own. Somehow, she managed it, and from all accounts she was a virtuous, respected, and a proper lady. I have never heard anyone say anything but good about her.

Our grandmother Tasia was not only a wonderful mother but poetically gifted. When she was a young girl, she and her friend would walk and walk, and only speak in poetics. Some of us have a bit of that gift. But nothing like our beloved grandmother; certainly not me. Our late brother, Danny, came closest. I emphasize beloved because our grandmother was kind, resourceful and dedicated to her family, including her daughter's family.

From the early years of World War II and the subsequent Greek Civil War, when starvation was ravaging Greece, anything and everything she owned of value, she sold to obtain monies and give to my mother so that our family could avoid starvation. There are numerous stories of less fortunate families in that era who suffered greatly from starvation and eventually died. One individual of that era was recently on a Greek channel and advised that his family was so poor that due to extreme hunger, he was losing all his teeth, and, on the touch, they felt as soft as gums!

For a period, our grandmother also had our oldest sister Dina and after Dina, our brother Ted stay with her. The principal objective of these moves was to allow the family to survive severe times of hunger and for our grandmother to have company. Also, older children like Dina could and did help our grandmother with chores.

Although I have no recollection of meeting my grandmother when I lived in Kefalonia, based on a photo that is included in this book, as well as stories shared by my siblings, I met her several times between birth and up to five or six years of age. In the mid-1050s, she departed for Panama to live with her second son, Vasilios.

My first recollection of our grandmother, Anastasia was in the mid-1960s. This is when we lived at 821 S. Lyman Avenue, Oak Park, Illinois. This was the first home we owned in America. It was a wonderful bi-level stucco home with a full and finished basement. We were and are grateful at the opportunities this great nation made available to us. Our grandmother arrived from Panama and stayed for a few of months to visit and catch up with our mother and family. She must have been in her mid-seventies when she visited. Then she returned to Greece and lived the remainder of her life with her first-born son, Christophoros and family. They all resided in the village of their birth at their house in Frangata.

A fond memory I have of our grandmother is her daily walks up and down our block. She was kind and respective to all. In fact, every person she met she would enthusiastically greet with a warm *"kalimera sas!"* a respectful "good morning" in Greek. The memory is deeply embedded in my mind, since most of the "people" greeted were trees planted by the City of Oak Park, in front of every home on the block. The dear, dear lady was primarily blind. Even so, she never forgot to be cordial. I was fortunate to meet our maternal grandmother once again when I visited Kefalonia in 1971. I had just finished college and after four arduous years of university and prior to seeking gainful employment, I thirsted for a little break and to enjoy and rediscover the beauty of the island that a long time ago I called home.

Sadly, upon my return in 1971, our grandmother, in her mid-eighties, was now totally blind. I gave her a hug and kissed her on the cheek. She looked completely disoriented and lost. Although my uncle, his family and I, repeatedly advised her, I do not believe our beloved grandmother knew who I was.

During my visit, I was respective but somewhat indifferent, possibly a bit uncomfortable and do not think that I showed the proper compassion she so richly deserved. After a while she was taken to her room to rest. In retrospect, I wish I had known more of her past. I deeply regret I was not more mature, empathetic, and engaging. Just a naive young man who knew next to nothing about life and its various twists and turns. I should have shown more love and respect for this great lady! After a few years went by, we were advised that this saintly person had passed. She was probably in her late eighties or early nineties. True to her disposition, despite all her suffering, I never once heard her complain.

Another story about the Civil War era involved my grandmother asking her nephew Dionisi, who is better known by his nickname, "Riganas," to take an expensive table setting to Argostoli and sell it. Our grandmother's objective was to give the monies received from the sale to my mother to feed her children. Riganas returned empty handed and advised my grandmother that on the way to the city, he slipped, and all the plates and cutlery were destroyed. Nothing remained so there was no money to give. She did not believe him and accused him of lying. He kicked our grandmother and verbally abused her. She responded by cursing him and saying, "May you lose the leg that kicked me." I am not a believer of curses, but my uncle did in fact lose that leg by stepping on a minefield. I am certain my grandmother said this in time of extreme anger due to the extreme stress brought forth by the difficult times.

I met my uncle in his late years, and he appeared to be a good man. He went on to raise two handsome men and three beautiful and kind daughters. All married with children, respected by all that know them and live productive and happy lives here in America. They are fine relatives. In fact, I have baptized one of his granddaughters, Angela Hilas, now Angela Garbis. She has grown up to be a beautiful and kind person, excellent mother and wife. Angela is married to Denny Garbis. A likeable, hardworking person, but not a relative, at least not in the modern era. He is, though, from the village of Frangata.

Finally, from all that I have heard from siblings and others who knew our grandmother, Anastasia, she deserves a statute to be erected in her honor by the children of Gerasimos and Arsinoe Garbis; at minimum, to be revered and never forgotten. Based on my empirical inquiries, I am a believer!

Pavlatae

The Pavlatae are the relatives to whom many of us owe much. They were and are smart, bold, and industrious. Note that this is my grandmother's side and Nikola's wife. I do not know much about my grandma Ekaterini except as previously mentioned—she was on the tall side as were her two brothers that I met. My grandmother's brother Gerasimos and his wife, Stella, brought to America my father, his brother, Spiro, and at least another niece and nephew—Koula Garbis and Michalis Pavlatos. All four were first cousins. Koula was the younger sister of my uncle Thanasi, John Garbis's father. All are good and kind people and with their spouses, raised fine and responsible children.

Another brother of my grandmother's was also in the States. His name was Athanasios (Thanasi) Pavlatos. Younger brother of Gerasimos and Andreas who was the oldest. As previously noted, Andreas came to America first and then brought the other two brothers. He worked along with Gerasimos and Thanasi and other Greek immigrants laying railroad tracks in Montana. They slept in the rail cars. At some point Andreas, returned to Kefalonia. Gerasimos and Thanasi stayed and eventually ended up in Chicago. There is a possibility that before Chicago, they lived for a period in the state of Michigan and may have owned a bar there.

Both Gerasimos and Athanasios were successful businessmen. Both were probably around their late sixties when we arrived. Clearly Gerasimos, at least in his older stage, appeared to be significantly more prosperous and polished. Both were very good and supportive uncles and relatives. Both, financially sound. Thanasis, in the 1960s, loaned my brother Anthony $5,000 to open a grocery store at Central and Lake Street. That would probably translate to providing Tony with roughly $50,000 in today's monies. And he did so willingly! My father interceded on Tony's behalf. Anthony, industrious as he was, paid him back within a year.

Gerasimos' wife, Aunt Stella was beautiful, kind, vivacious and highly likeable. She was very approachable and smiled easily. Any amounts of encomiums regarding our aunt's demeanor in life would be insufficient. Individuals with such attributes are rare. We were blessed to have had her as one of our own.

Gerasimos and Stella had three children: Michael, Chris and Marinela in that order. Chris has become a prime surgeon and for a while worked as an orthopedic specialist for the Chicago Bears. Michael obtained a degree in accounting and has a successful accounting practice. Marinela is a beautiful person and also in the professional field. As her siblings, she also took after her parents—she is kind, gracious, and was blessed to have her mother's smile. Like their parents before them, all are fine and respected people. Also, as their parents before them, they respect relatives and do not trouble or speak ill of anyone. In fact, just the opposite.

My father shared with me how my uncle Gerasimos met his wife Stella who at that time, lived in Athens. He was walking by a beach near Athens, when he saw this gorgeous young woman, bubbly and funny and was immediately smitten. He was, I believe, roughly twenty years her senior. Irrespective of age differential, they were certainly compatible and a couple to admire. A few years after the passing of her husband, she, too, passed. Sadly, cancer was the cause. I visited her at the hospital. She was too far gone and filled with morphine. I kissed her forehead and told her I loved her and wished her well. I still remember, as a young boy visiting with my family their plush home by California and Foster Avenue. New Year's or a celebratory holiday or just getting together were usually the reasons. They were always kind and generous.

My uncle Gerasimos held a party for his four-year-old daughter, Marinela. At a banquet hall. At least for Greeks, having a large celebration at a banquet hall is usually because of weddings or wedding engagements or christenings. He confided in my parents and other relatives that he did this because of his age. He acknowledged that chances of him being alive when Marinela would become of age were remote and would not be around to see his beloved daughter get married. If my recollection is correct, my uncle passed not too much later after that celebration. Certainly, way before Marinela was of marital age. I have not met anyone of our relatives or friends who speak of them with ill will. This speaks volumes for their classy behavior. We should all aspire to emulate the behavior of these Pavlatae!

In regard to Thanasi Pavlatos, about the same time as his brother, he also married a Greek girl from Athens. Her name was Mary. She was a schoolteacher from a good family. To back track, both brothers were probably in their late fifties or early sixties. They returned to Greece to marry a Greek girl. That was not unique, especially in that period. Greeks were still new to America, and assimilation was very slow in coming. As was Stella, Mary was considerably younger than my uncle. And as noted, In the years after the wars, poverty and starvation were in abundance for most of the population of Greece. Looking back in that era, it was not unusual for Greeks in their later years, having made a decent a living in the States, having steady jobs, even as dishwashers, to return to Greece and marry a girl at least half their age. They called those "successful" Greeks from America "Brooklides." I assume a derivation of the city of Brooklyn, thinking all Greeks lived in Brooklyn, and most importantly, they have lots of money.

This type of marriage arrangement is now considered at best a very bad idea for many good and practical reasons. At that time, if you lived in America, the locals were in awe of their American success, as a drachma was hard to find, let alone a US dollar! Most importantly, it is not difficult to surmise the motivation for the parents was that by "sacrificing "their young and beautiful daughter she would be financially sound and not exposed to starvation or need of a dowry, which was difficult to come by in those trying times. Just as important, in that era, families had many children, one thought must have been that their daughter and new husband would be able to bring their siblings to the States for a better life. More than not, they did.

My aunt Stella was lucky that she had a good man and measured spouse. She was very lucky and so was my uncle. But as many found a decent life and happiness, probably just as many felt as if they were in bondage. My uncle Thanasi was, at least, in his elder years a bit unusual regarding the handling of his wife. It is my understanding that he would lock Mary in the hotel room that they were staying and would go to work. When he returned, probably late in the day, he would unlock the door. I understand that the girl finally had enough and was able to get out of the room by jumping out of the window. I assume, he never saw her again.

This is so unlike what you would expect from a quality relative; and Thanasi was that and more. Nice man, but apparently, in his older years, had an issue with trusting women. If so, why marry this young girl? This saddens us, and I wish Mary nothing but the best, wherever she may be. I hope she forgave this man, who I trust was not the real Athanasios of his youth.

Recently, I was contacted via Ancestry.com that I have a second cousin who claimed to be Athanasis's granddaughter. Her name is Lewanda (Lee) Pavlatos Hinton. She knew of Athanasi, Gerasimos, and Stella. She also knew his date of birth, which was in 1881. Based on my grandmother Ekaterini's age, it sounded right. My uncle Thanasi must have a decent-sized family tree in America but not by Mary who he probably married right after the Greek Civil War (late 1940s). Based on the information and subsequent discussion with Lee, Thanasi was married to her grandmother, a non-Greek, in 1921—a girl of English and German descent. This was confirmed by two sources: Anthony, my brother, and Mike, my cousin, the firstborn of Gerasimos and Stella.

Lee and I eventually spoke. She lives in Arizona. She advised that her grandmother left my uncle because he was a bit too stern and on occasion hit her. She got pregnant with a son, Lee's father. When her father (Thanasis's son) married her mother, unbeknown to her mother, Thanasi's son was already married and had two kids. Lee's mother and father had three kids, she, being one of the three.

Lee recalls that her father was very violent with her mother. Out of fear of her life and the life of her children, she ran way and send each child to a different foster home. Lee attributes her father's violent behavior due to his service as a paratrooper in World War II. He fought in every major battle, including the Battle of the Bulge. By every account, a very bloody and hard-fought battle. Clearly, he was a war hero. Unfortunately, after too many close calls, he probably may have not been 100 percent. After what he experienced, who could blame him.

The bottom line: Thanasi has at least five grandchildren from his son. One can only wonder how many great grandchildren!! Just as important, at least Lee and her children know who their great grandfather was and just as important, they know that they have relatives!

Vasilios Kourouklis

Vasilios Kourouklis was my grandmother's second child from her one and only husband Peter. As previously noted, my grandfather Peter passed relatively young. Probably in his late twenties or early thirties. My grandmother never remarried. Christophoros was the firstborn. My mother Arsinoe was the youngest of the three.

My son, Christopher Jeramiah (I call him Jeramiah or J), was named after our uncle Christophoros and my father. I met my uncle once. This was when I graduated from the University of Illinois, Chicago Campus, and went to Kefalonia when I was twenty-one years old. I met and very much liked Uncle Christophoros and his family. He was a kind man, as was his family. But the older I became, and with the passing of my father, I realized it was a mistake for me not to singularly honor my father. Although he is baptized as Christopher Jeramiah, I always call him "Gerasimos" (Jeramiah or J).

It is my understanding that Vasili and our mother, Arsinoe, were very close, as both loved to dance and sing. Vasili had a pleasant and accomplished tenor voice; my mom liked to sing but did not have a singing voice. Regrettably, much as I loved my mom, I wish, I did not inherit her singing abilities. I love to sing, and regrettably, I sound good only in the shower. I do not think there is a microphone around that I can chameleonize and make my untrained and hoarse voice better.

That is the sad fact. Nevertheless, I still sing. I cannot help it. It is like asking a canary that was born to sing to stop singing-*even if his voice is cacophonous, he cannot*!

If Phyllis and I are blessed with grandchildren, my wish and hope is that at least one of my grandchildren will have my passion and soulfulness, but with a beautiful voice like some of my relatives. They will touch hearts and lives and make a difference. Something that I yearned for but could never achieve!

As previously mentioned, besides my uncle Vasilios Kourouklis, a cousin of ours on my grandmother Anastasia's side, Father Ioanis Mesolouras has a phenomenal voice. He can sing anything and do it like no one else. He sounds and as he aged, looks like Pavoratti. He is also a class act. In fact, as a young man in his early twenties, he would take my mother, at that time old and legally blind down by our beach to enjoy the waters of her younger years. If that isn't class and compassion, I do not know what is.

Vasili fought in World War I against the Turks. Greece entered this war in 1917 by invading Smyrna. It is my understanding that King Konstandine and the Prime Minister Venizelos were in conflict as to whether to join the German side or the English and French side in this war. Venizelos was for joining the English and French; the King wanted to side with the Germans. The King lost a referendum and was exiled. For a period, the war was successful, and the Greeks occupied Smyrna. At that time, Smyrna had over six hundred thousand Greek inhabitants. This was a bit more than the population of Athens.

The king's son, Alexander, who was amiable to the Venizelos regime, became the king of Greece, and all was going well at the Turkish front. Allegedly, a monkey bit and poisoned him, resulting in his death. This seems to be too surreal to be true. But, as far as I can ascertain, no one questioned his death. King Constantine was then recalled. He and Venizelos, despite the success achieved by the Greek army, renewed their feud in reference to war strategy. A referendum was declared to determine who should govern Greece: King Konstantine or Venizelos. It is my understanding that the referendum required the fighting to cease for about two months to allow for voting to take place and determine who the population preferred: the king or the prime minister. This unwise decision to delay and cease fighting allowed the Turks to recalibrate. Concurrently, since the king won, and Venizelos lost, he was exiled. With Venizelos exiled, most, if not all, of the senior generals resigned. As a result, a very good Turkish general, Kamal, then turned the tide.

The resignations of most or all the seasoned generals left all the inexperienced officers in charge. It appears that this caused the English and French to lose faith, and lost their desire to assist the argumentative Greeks. Also, it did not help our cause that the Greeks wanted to continue the war and capture Ankara which is located far east from the Aegean Shores. This was not an objective of their allies. It would have been stupid for Greeks to continue, but they did. Consequently, the war was lost at a tremendous cost of life and gifted a dismal future to the Greek nation's posterity, which has yet to recover from.

The Greek leadership forgot their ancestors' sage advice: "A measured step is the best step." They forgot how a unified phalanx of old was so affective but one that was not properly structured would crumble. They became intoxicated with their initial victories against the Turkish forces, became arrogant and self-serving. Instead of using the war to build a strong foundation for its people, King and Prime Minister squandered the Greek nation's future by being petty with in-house fighting. By doing so, they forgot their principal objective—take back what was taken from them a long time ago. They squandered the opportunity to utilize the re-acquired territory for its inhabitants and provide Greece with a long-term projectory of a more industrious, powerful, and self-sustaining nation. How sad, how stupid, and how selfish to put your personal objectives first and not your nation's!

The brutality of the Turkish army on the Greeks in Smyrna has been well documented. Also, when the war was being lost, the population of Smyrna who could, was trying to escape the brutality and slaughter of the Turkish soldiers by swimming or boating to the English ships, stationed by the port of Smyrna. The English did not allow the refugees to board. This despite knowing well of the brutality and carnage for which Turks were known. In other words, for whatever reasons, the allies became enemies and violently with the use of clubs, etc., forced the Greeks to return to shore or drown. The Turkish army, true to its reputation, did not disappoint.

For almost a year after the end of the war, my uncle Vasili did not return home, and the military could not locate his whereabouts and presumed him dead. In fact, he sustained a leg wound. The French army came upon him and turned him over to the Turkish army. When the war ended and there was a prisoner exchange, Vasili was allowed to return to his homeland.

On the annual anniversary of his death, my mother, then in her teens, and my grandmother, both dressed in black, where going to church for his memorial. They were shocked and extremely happy to see Vasili alive. To my mother and grandmother, it must have felt like Lazarus being brought back from the dead!

As noted, Vasilis was the young man who defended our grandfather Nikolas against the three brothers who bullied him. That scuffle must have occurred after he returned from the war. After that confrontation, the three brothers attempted to ambush and kill Vasili. He was smart and coy. He used to sleep on a "tree bed" when he worked his fields. Expecting an ambush, Vasili put together hay or grass in a sack and placed his hat where his head would be. Sure enough, someone took a shot thinking he was asleep. After hearing of the above, my grandmother begged Vasili to leave Kefalonia. She advised him that she had already lost her husband; she was not about to lose her son. Vasili heeded her advice and went to Athens.

While in Athens, he worked as a street merchant singing while selling combs and other trinkets. A woman of means who got to know him, asked if he would be able to come to her house and sing at a party she was hosting. Vasili gladly accepted. He must have been impressive because after the party the appreciative host inquired what, if anything, she could do for him. He asked if she could send him to the West. She did as he wished, and put Vasili on a frigate whose destination was Panama.

With his wit, charm, and song, he first sold coffee grinds on the streets of Panama—supposedly mixed with fine dirt to increase profit. He eventually ended up in the canal zone, where he bought or started a restaurant. At that time, the Americans controlled the canal zone, and therefore it fell under US jurisdiction. Not surprising, being personable, Americans liked him, and he was paid in dollars. Vasili became wealthy. My uncle sent for my mother's first husband to join him, and Panagiotis Markadonatos did. Tragedy occurred, and Panagiotis never made it back to his family.

As the story goes, Vasili got into a fray with a customer. Panagiotis got in the middle to stop it and apparently was fatally stabbed. Not certain we shall ever know the complete truth except that because of this incident, he died. After her father's death, my eldest sister Dina remembered a quick trip to Greece by Vasili. She recalled that he had our mother sign documents and then promptly returned to Panama. Do not know nor do I wish to conjecture the purpose of this visit.

With the above background, Vasili and family, Kate (wife), sons Peter, Nick and George and Daughter Anastasia (Tasia) returned to Greece from Panama for an extended vacation around 1946. At the time the Greek Civil War was ravaging Greece and its people. It is estimated that he visited Kefalonia with $100,000 or more. For that amount of money, in those times, he could have bought much of Kefalonia. Its purchasing power magnified by the extreme poverty and destitute of this little nation. Furthermore, even in America, $100,000 in 1946 probably equated to more than $1,000,000 in today's exchange rate.

My mother, holding in her arms her son Bill, named in honor of my uncle, went to greet her beloved brother and family as they disembarked from their ship at Argostoli. This is Kefalonia's key seaport and capital city. Bill was less than a year old. This giant of person who was now famous and justifiably, the toast of his village, upon seeing his sister, instantaneously became small in demeanor and thinking. Despite being siblings and close in their youth, the death of her husband due to his actions or inaction, as well as the prevalent starvation occurring in Greece, he advised his sister that he did not know her and walked away. His family followed suit.

I cannot imagine my mother's surprise and pain experienced by this unexpected rejection. The shunning, I surmise was because my mother married a man below her status—albeit Greeks, by nature, are egalitarians, nor was there a caste system in Greece. Furthermore, before he became wealthy in Panama, he was as poor as anyone in Kefalonia. That is why he was a singing street vendor in Athens; and that is why he asked a wealthy benefactress to help him find his fortune overseas. Apparently, his new status in life blocked out that part of his life. Maybe he had his reasons, but even if he did, it does not justify this cruel and callous behavior toward his sister and her family in these very, very difficult and dangerous times, especially since the two oldest were the children of the man who died in his arms.

I recall three additional disappointing stories advised to me by my siblings of my uncle's return to Kefalonia:

- Although my family, at that period was in dire straits and very poor, he totally ignored them. He did not once try to be courteous to his sister, brother-in-law or nephews and nieces. As noted, two of those, Dina and Denny were the children of the man who died in his arms. When the opulent Panamanian and family would drive by in their jeep, my siblings would be on the lookout, see them coming as they turned by the Megalos Giros, (about a mile away) and would hustle up from their home and line up by the main street to say hi, hoping for a gift, a hello, or just an acknowledgment from their rich and famous uncle. His family would throw some candy as if they were dogs looking for a snack, never acknowledging them as they drove by and kept going the same fast speed. Our uncle was probably driving to Lourdata. This was his spouse's hometown and is located east, adjacent to our village, Vlachata. Lourdata is also located near the coast and has an excellent view of the coastline's natural beauty. To all other relatives and friends, my uncle was generous to an extreme. He bought one of his godsons a brand-new car! Other friends and relatives, received monies, and gifts. He was sought after and became a godfather to several children of friends and relatives. Always being generous to a fault.

- My parents were never giving one iota of thought to receiving assistance. Recall, this part of the story is post World War II and in the middle of the Civil War. It was extremely bloody and lasted for over three years, officially ending in late 1949. People were regularly dying of hunger and emaciation. Our family was not an exception. If it was not for my father, and the older siblings' extraordinary hard work who were fortunate to find jobs, as well as my grandmother Anastasia selling all she had, dying by starvation was not an unreasonable expectation. On the plus side, they had a lot of friends and neighbors in that same situation, so they did have each other's shoulders to lean on!

In these desperate times, my father sadly, killed an Italian soldier who was holding a donkey. He would not give the donkey to my father. I assume the soldier had taken the donkey from a local. After a few back-and-forths, as the soldier was not willing to give up the animal, my father shot and killed him. Our family ate the donkey. When my mother learned what she was eating, she threw up! Although this sounds disgusting to us, the English slaughtered over four hundred thousand of their prized war horses in World War I to feed their hungry soldiers.

Bottom line: there is no good justification for killing in this case. But I cannot place judgment, as I was not in his shoes with so many mouths to feed and a meal nowhere to be found. These were desperate time, during which a morsel of food could determine who lived and who died. Finally, the Italian was a soldier of the invading army who had just lost the war. Otherwise, I do not believe my father would have shot him. It was not in his makeup. This I know.

- Just before New Year's, my father asked Dionisi, my eldest brother and the son of Peter, who got killed on his watch, to ask his uncle if he could borrow our father thirty drachmas (probably about thirty dollars in today's currency, maybe a bit more) so that he could buy meat and food for the holiday, and he would pay him back next week. The quest for a loan was necessary because as you may recall, Denny went to play cards and lost the thirty drachmas owed to my father for work performed. My uncle arrogantly goose-stepped back and forth like a German general and asked my brother as he stood, "If I give you the thirty drachmas, do I have your word that *your* father will pay me back next week? My brother said yes, and he got the thirty drachmas. It was promptly paid back the following week. Dionisi was about fourteen years old. And again, the son of the man who supposedly died in his arms.

A Heartfelt Tribute to Dickie, Our Best and Dearest Friend

Our father came to America, and after a few years he was able to bring the rest of us. In the meantime, he did send monies, and we built a comfortable little home. For a couple of years or so, we lived well. When it was hot, some of us slept on the roof, which was flat and cemented. It was finished in a way that additional floors could be built if desired. I assume this was the plan since we did have a big family, and the wall emanating from the foundation was about one foot higher than the flat cement roof. On one of those nights, it was pitch dark as there were no lights in the village and I went to sleep on the roof. I saw a shooting star. It was a beautiful and an unforgettable sight.

When it was time to depart for America, we hugged and said our goodbyes to our beloved dog, Dickie. We got into the taxi to take us to the ferry boat. Poor Dickie kept trying to jump in the car and whimpered continuously, begging to come with us. He was at a loss as to why we were leaving; and a bigger loss as to why he was not coming with. After all, we grew up with Dickie, and he was family through and through.

Our family had arranged with my brother-in-law Toto and Dina, who lived close by in the village of Mousata (about a mile west of our village), to take Dickie to stay with them. That was the plan. But our

Dickie would have none of that. Every time Dickie was taken to Toto's and Dina's house, he would leave and go back to our house's veranda, waiting, waiting, and waiting. This went on for a long time. Unfortunately, that day never came for our beloved friend and protector.

After much suffering, Dickie had become bitter and unruly. He was mercifully poisoned to take him out of his misery. The poison may have terminated our Dickie's life. But he died long before due to a broken heart. The poison was a blessing, as it terminated his suffering.

Young as I was, I never thought much about Dickie until my late thirties and progressively more as I aged. Now there isn't a day that passes that I do not think of this loyal, dear friend that we left behind. And when I do, my heart is heavy with pain, and my eyes moisten for the immense suffering he must have endured due to losing his family. It feels so wrong and unjust, and it was! Dogs and many other animals have deep feelings and love for those who raised and took care of them. Unfortunately, bringing Dickie to America was not viable or an option.

When I was blessed with a family of my own and bought a house in Naperville, Phyllis and I went looking for a dog. A dear friend of mine and mentor in claims administration, James Nesci, advised that yellow Labs were very friendly and great with kids. We purchased a puppy that we named Peaches. When I picked Peaches and raised her over my head to greet her, I became slightly emotional when I looked into Peaches' eyes. I was thinking of the friend who we left behind. Purchasing Peaches was a way to say I have not forgotten you, my dearest friend, nor will I ever. A boy's bond with his dog is just too strong to be broken or forgotten.

"Peaches" was the name Phyllis gave to our new puppy. She saw her in a dream and said to the puppy, "You look so beautiful—yellow and a girl! I will call you Peaches." Of course, Peaches in the dream looked like the Peaches in real life. Most yellow Labs look alike. We were first advised that we would have a yellow Lab at the next birthing, around Christmas. Then we got a call in October advising that a baby Lab was available. Peaches was born on July 20—the same day as the name day that is celebrated in honor of the Prophet Elias (also my name day).

CHAPTER 7

Leaving for America

After we left with the limousine, we got on a ferry at a seaport on the eastern part of Kefalonia called Kilini and went to Athens. Upon our arrival in Athens, we stayed in the suburb of Holargos, not too far from Athens. My brother-in-law Toto had a sister living in Holargos. Her name was Marousa. We were her and her family's guests for a week or two. Then we rented a place for a couple of months until we were able to depart for America. She had one daughter (Emilia) and two sons (Takis and Eleftherios). The sons were older than me and closer to my siblings ages. The daughter was closer to my age. They were all very kind and hospitable to us. After a month or two, we were able to board a four propeller TWA to come to America. There was a stop in Germany. I'm not certain of the name of the city, but I am guessing Hamburg. Irrespective, that city greatly impressed us. As we never, ever saw so many trains in one place and so many train tracks. My aunt Marianthi, the spouse of my uncle Spiro, also accompanied us to America.

Recall that our father and uncle Spiro were sponsored by my uncle Gerasimos Pavlatos and his spouse, Stella. Our father advised me that for the first few months in America he and my uncle would share a closet as a bedroom. One slept during the daytime. The other during the night. Apparently, that was viable due to different work shifts.

When we boarded in Athens, each family was given twenty-five dollars so they could take an orphaned baby to America and deliver it to its adoptive parents. I do not recall our baby boy's name. I do know that when we landed we gave the orphan to his new parents. We were all sad to see him go. He was too. This little boy became especially attached to my brother Anthony. We hope he found excellent parents and has a fruitful, happy, and long life in America.

Our aunt Marianthi was given a child who would not stop crying, and it was driving her to the edge. This was a very long flight from Greece to Germany, to England and finally America; all stops in a propeller airplane. Still, she dutifully cuddled and comforted the child as best as she could. My guess is that our aunt was delighted when she finally delivered this infant to its adoptive parents. TWA was if not the biggest, one of the larger and more popular international airlines in those days. The plane we boarded had four propellers. There were commercial jets at that time, but they weren't yet widely used.

As previously noted, after Germany, we stopped briefly in England, prior to commencing our long flight to New York. When we departed from England, the first hours of the flight were serene and comforting. Sunny day and just a few clouds. In fact, it was so nice that the pilot was considerate and provided us with a better visual. He flew lower than usual when he spotted a ship in the Atlantic. The sun was bright, waters calm, and the view of the Atlantic Ocean was beautiful, and we were waiving to the ship and its travelers.

Unfortunately, this did not last. At some point we encountered a hurricane. Because it was propeller driven, the airplane could not fly high enough above the clouds to avoid the hurricane's violent turbulence. As a result, we experienced severe and nonstop ups and downs for a very long time. It was like an elevator that continuously went from the first floor to the one hundredth floor abruptly, rapidly, and nonstop. People were throwing up and pleading with Saint Gerasimos, the Virgin Mary, and other saints who were specific to each traveler's place of birth to save them.

I have confirmed with my older brothers that two of the four propellers stopped working. Also, water was dripping in the plane! For my part, I recall, being very quiet, frozen and looking at distressed people all around. I must have been petrified with terror. Finally, I joined the chorus. I do not know how long it was before we landed but it seemed like eternity. Although I thought we landed in New York as planned, Tony corrected me and advise that due to the storm, the plane was diverted to Canada. When we landed, it was still rainy and dark but the hurricane was far behind. We gave the pilot a huge, well-earned ovation. Landing was in the dark, so it could have been night or very early morning. Thankfully, no high winds. We then departed for our next destination via train or bus to New York.

When we arrived In New York, we were given a red apple and half a bologna sandwich with American cheese. After taking one bite, I told my mother in Greek, "This taste like shit! I'm going to starve in America!" As I am sure you have surmised, I now eat cold cuts of most type, pizza, Chinese and Japanese food, etc. Funny how one's palate changes and adopts to their surroundings. Even so, being from the village, to this day I will not eat meat unless it is well done, and thank you, but no sushi!

From New York, we took the train to Chicago, where we were met by our father and our brother Danny. Danny jumped ship at either New York or New Orleans and found his way to Chicago. He then married Rosalia, which made him legal. Rosalia was about ten years older than Denny, very kind, and pretty. The older I got, and the better acquainted we became, I considered Rosalia a saint. Always agreeable and always kind to all. Rosalia had a brother and mother who lived in Chicago. Their last name was Paris. We met both. After that meeting, I do not recall seeing them again. They appeared to have been good people. If my memory serves me right, the mother had a kind face and on the thin side; the brother was on the tall side, and his hair cut short.

Kedzie and Washington

The first place we lived in Chicago was by Kedzie and Washington. This was in late 1958. This appeared to be a well-maintained, predominantly Black neighborhood. Although we met black people when we wondered out of the house, we never experienced anything but kindness from them.

I remember meeting my sister-in-law Rosa and little Arsinoe. She must have been a few months old and in her crib. I do not recall anything noteworthy, except one thing. At least once, my mother and father got into a huge argument. My mother left the house. My father asked me to find her and bring her back. I walked and found her by this lake not too far away. This lake was very well designed and manicured, with small boats available for rental. In its heyday (1930s and 1940s), I assume it was a very popular spot. I found my mother sitting by the water and kept asking her in Greek to please come home. After beseeching her for a while she returned with me. This might have happened more than once. Not certain of the cause of these arguments.

At Kedzie and Washington is when I first saw shows and movies on TV. There was the Lawrence Welk Show that had couples dancing as part of their show. When the girls would twirl, their short fluffy dresses would rise and one could see their underwear. I would close my eyes in embarrassment. Another show, perhaps *I Love Lucy*, would have a character whose last name was "Mr. Moony." When in the show someone would call out "Mr. Moooony!" my mother would break out in a hearty laugh. As I subsequently learned, that word in Greek is a slang term for the female private part! Not a word to use. We also watched the then very popular shows *Bonanza* and *Lassie*. My dad would tell me that because *Lassie* was about a young boy and his dog, it would remind him of his son Ilias and our dog Dickie. One of the two joined him in America.

Congress and Van Buren

After a few months, we moved to a first-floor apartment by Cicero and Van Buren. We lived there for two and possibly three years. After a short time, my mother was asked by the same brother, Vasili, if we could take in his oldest son, Dimitri. He was taking classes at a nearby university to study philosophy. I do not recall the name of this institution. My parents acquiesced. They were never offered compensation for shelter or food or ever asked—or probably ever wanted.

Dimitri was not a bad person. He had some bad and perhaps a couple of abnormal habits. One of them was that he would often come home late and intoxicated. After a short period staying with us, Dimitri got into an argument with my brothers Ted and Tony, and blows were exchanged. At the end of this short exchange, Dimitiri began to inconsolably cry. He held a large knife to his stomach, threatening to kill himself. I recall being next to my mother who was trying to console him. Dimitri soon after this weird episode went to live on his own.

At Cicero and Van Buren, we made many friends of various ages, including Dick Strable and his family (German), Pat Ross (Irish), who was Bill's age, and a Greek boy, Tony, Bill's age. If I recall correctly,

Tony was from the neighboring island of Zakinthos. Tony was short and muscular, good-looking, personable and friendly. He also raised Pidgeon's on the roof of a three or four floor apartment building that he and family were renting space in. My brother Bill was a bit too wild for Tony's taste, so they never got close.

It was a vibrant neighborhood with many young folks. All pretty much friends and played street baseball in our alley, water fights, even camping with Tony and friends on a bushy parcel of land that was west of and very close to May School. It was 1959, when the White Sox were a very good team. The shortstop's name was Louie Aparicio. So, when we played street ball, my friends would call me Louie, in honor of the great shortstop. Perhaps this was the trigger that made me a White Sox fan.

My brother mentioned to our neighbors, the Strables, that he had a tough younger brother. Not certain why he did; I am guessing they discussed younger brothers. Somehow it was arranged that I would wrestle Dick. Dick was probably about two years or older than me, and as I found out, no pushover. We wrestled in his backyard, with his mother and the rest of the family sitting on their back porch cheering him on. In my youthful memory, the match seemed to have lasted for quite a while. Maybe because Dick was not easy to subdue or due to a young boy's magnified memory. Dick's mother was old, normal height, and heavy. Her voice carried ominously. The memory of an old woman screaming loudly tells me that she was relentless in her directives for Dick to "get him" and win. If Dick would have lost, I think he would have been in serious trouble.

For what seemed a lengthy period, we were able to get out of each other's holds, take the advantage then lose the advantage. Eventually, he got me in a hold that had me pinned with my stomach down and was pressing and twisting one of my legs. I tried but could not get out. Either I would be subdued or break a leg. My brother told me to say, "I give." I did and lost. Nevertheless, there was always respect and affinity between us. The Strables lived on the same block about six houses west of us.

Oak Park

After a couple of years, with the strong backing of my two older brothers—Ted and Tony—my father was able to afford a decent home in the village of Oak Park. Most likely, it was totally the brothers' deposit money, as the father did not make much and was paying for the normal and other family expenses—for example, to build a home in Kefalonia, to bring us to America, rent an apartment, buy food, send me to Greek school, and more. To their credit and class, my brothers never shared with me their contributions. Only in my later years did I become curious and ask how our father could afford a down payment, as he was probably making, at that time, about $150 per week. Although a good salary for that time, it would never be sufficient enough to allow our father to save for a down payment.

On a separate topic, guess who came to live with us in Oak Park for an extended period of about six months? Having squandered all the wealth he had accumulated, our uncle Vasilios and family moved to America. He needed a place to stay until he was able to establish himself and asked if he could stay with us.

My father was a better man than I will ever be. He acquiesced and my uncle and aunt Kathy, his wife, stayed with us. After six months, not only was it getting thin for my father but also unaffordable. My uncle and wife were asked and moved out. He opened a coffee shop, which was a place for playing cards and gambling. Unfortunately, the shop was unsuccessful. It is a shame that a man who rose so high did not live a measured life and fell so steeply down. If I had to guess, probably due to gambling issues.

His son Pano stayed in Panama. It was rumored he eventually became a radio announcer. When we first met him, he was tall, serious, and handsome. We were told he was an ambassador for Panama; I do not recall for which country.

My uncle's youngest child, George, a good guy, appears to have committed suicide and is survived by two sons. I understand they have become wonderful gentlemen and live in Kefalonia, near their mother. Nikolaos and I, despite at least a ten-year difference, became good friends and had fun together. He was and is a good man. Although we do not talk or see each other much, we are still friends. He has one son and three daughters. All are beautiful and have married well. I never discuss his father. You cannot blame the children for a parent's ill deeds. My cousins all appear to be and have been good people. Looking back, I admire my father for being magnanimous, forgiving the unforgivable, a noble spirit, and not being a small person.

When I first met my uncle Vasili, he was my hero. I knew nothing of his past, and he was likeable. Tough guy him, tough guy me, defender of the weak; me too. Loved to sing—me too, but not well, not even close. But after I became aware of all the stuff that transpired in Kefalonia, and although I was not yet born when he came to Greece, I became bitter and had a hard time forgiving him for his cruelty toward my family in such difficult times.

I know it is wrong to be so rigid. You can hurt me, and I will almost always forgive you. Hurt those I love—different story. But maybe it is time to move on. My uncle was a product of his time. He was very smart, bold and in his prime, a force to be reckoned with. Sadly, with his elevation in status, he forgot to remain humble, tolerant and forgiving. He allowed small things to muddy his logic and apparently, he was never able to see the bigger picture. Still, I am comfortable that much of what our grandmother Tasia sold to feed our family was gifted to her by our uncle Vasili and possibly Christopher. So, in a roundabout and unintended way, he did help the family in its darkest times.

Despite his late stage of life, probably in his late sixties, he performed two impressive stunts while he stayed with us. One was placing a hardened whole coconut on the ground and placed a matchbox underneath. He would then get on his knees and use his fist as a hammer. Upon impact, the coconut would explode. The other trick performed, I think, is much more difficult. He would take a fresh deck of cards in his two hands. He would twist them with both hands in an up-and-down motion rhythmically and in time cut them in half! I have no idea if it was skill or strength, but it was very impressive.

One final thought: Until recently, I would think about my uncle's callous behavior on a regular basis. It would bother me to no end. I would get upset and be unforgiving. Then, in mid-March 2020, on a Sunday morning, I went to our local church (Saint Athanasios), thinking about and troubled by my uncle's past behavior. As our priest delivered the liturgy, I looked at the front of the church, where painted on the wall is a huge iconography of our Lord's crucifixion. And instantly I recalled of how Christ, when he was on that cross and after being severely tortured and suffering with his last breath, pleaded with his father in heaven to "forgive them, for they know not what they do." I do not know why, but after that revelation, I felt sorry for my uncle and immediately forgave him. In doing so, I, too, have found peace.

CHAPTER 8

Epilogue

In the twilight of my life, my memory takes me back to those who I loved and loved me. To the times of my youth when we were all younger, naive, bold, and felt invincible. I look at the pictures of my youth and see certain people differently. Someone who I no longer recognize to be me, albeit I know it is. I smile with happiness when I look at the pictures of our family of years gone by when we were at our prime and all were healthy and lived to live. I yearn for that period, which I romanticize as if it were another Camelot reborn, and like Camelot, for some of us, it has long past to never return.

My memory takes me back to my ancestors of old and modern times. My heart and soul feel a strong longing for all, especially those we have prematurely lost and dearly miss, including our heartbreaking tragedies and the heavy price they or their families paid either by their actions or fate. For the mailman's daughter, the beautiful Reggina, nephew Peter M., niece Emily, and brother-in-law George. And recently, the loss of Dina, Bill, Denny, and Tony, albeit highly painful, easier to reconcile by the heart and mind. This is because they lived long enough that their families where stable, secure and mature. This cannot be said for the others.

I did not realize how caring and loving my family was, until I, too, became a father and husband, and learned their history and how hard they fought to keep us together and keep us alive. Until I wrote this book, I did not appreciate how hard my older brothers and father worked and what they went through in those severe economic times, brought forth by World War II and the Greek Civil War. No wonder Tony kept insisting for me to help him at his store. If he believed I owed him, he was 100 percent correct. In hindsight, I owed him much more than that. Being around him made me a better, wiser person. To all who preceded me, as long as my mind remains healthy, I shall never forget you nor the foundation you and our ancestors bestowed on us—respect, commitment, pride, hard work, honesty, sincerity, honor, and a desire to excel.

Sometimes we lose our way, and that is okay. It is human nature to challenge existing norms and deviate from the path we have been raised on. In many ways, these youthful rebellions are almost necessary to learn right from wrong and corresponding ramifications. Kind of your own personal boot camp. Even if it hurts, we must push on, and we must learn and be empowered through our difficult times. They will pass. And if you learn and become a better human being, it is worth it!

All of this would have had a different and probably not as good trajectory if it were not for our ancestors. All are special and all gave us their DNA which improved us. But the ones who must be especially acknowledged are the Pavlatae, who brought many nephews and nieces to America and allowed us to live the American dream! The descendants of those they brought to America, including yours truly, must never forget this special gift from this special family!

For me, personally, in my adult years, I have tried to be a man of honor, a good family man, and one who my family and ancestors can be proud of. My youthful years are a bit more nebulous and sketchier. Honor from a young boy's perception is not the same as that of an adult. It needs to simmer and hopefully, in time, he or she will acquire the desired attributes. Looking back on my younger years, I was no angel and made a myriad of mistakes with significant and sometimes costly ramifications. Consequently, out of ignorance, arrogance, self-righteousness, and naivety, I hurt many innocent and kind people. All of them meant something to me; some meant a great deal to me, and still do. Nothing was intentional. Just youthful naivety and indiscretions.

For those who I hurt, I am deeply sorry and wish I could go back in time and undo any action that caused this unintended harm. Unfortunately, that is not possible. I am sure I will continue to make mistakes, but *hopefully* they will be insignificant and not harmful. My salvation was that I converted my mistakes to experiences and became a *bit* wiser and hopefully a better person.

APPENDIX A

Battle of Mezenkert—a Brief Synopsis

The loss of Anatolia by the Greeks in World War I was not the most egregious self-serving behavior experienced by the Hellenes. A long time ago, a treacherous, treasonous, and self-serving behavior occurred at Byzantium, the precursor of modern Greece. This betrayal culminated in the defeat of a noble and brave emperor, Romanus Diogenes, by the Seljuk Turks on August 26, 1071, at the Battle of Mezenkert. If one looks at this battle closer, it was not his defeat. It was due to the wealthiest family in Byzantium, the Doukas family and their accomplices. The behavior of this family makes the series *Game of Thrones* look like child's play.

I urge anyone interested in history and who wishes to understand how the superpower of its time, after seven-hundred-plus years, became irrelevant in a relatively short period of time to pick up a copy of *A Short History of Byzantium* by the late historian John Norwich. It is an honest and revealing book that provides a comprehensive history of Byzantium and a detailed account of this battle. If you are of Greek descent, and you care about your people and its history, what is outlined will make you very upset. You will feel betrayed and painfully lament what could have been the future of Greece and its peoples.

If only key people in power had placed their love of Country first and not their ego or themselves, the future of Byzantium and Greece might have been very different. If they were forward looking with no blinders with the sole goal of country first, it would have been clear to them of Byzantium's future and potential disaster for all, including themselves and family! How blind, how sad, how stupid, and how criminal!

To make a long story short, after the death of an incompetent emperor named Constantine X Doukas, the empress widow, Eudocia, was asked to select the next emperor. The empress did not choose a Doukas or Doukas crony to replace the deceased emperor. She decided, instead, on Romanus Diogenes; as described by Norwich, "a handsome man who seemed to personify the military aristocracy". The Doukases and friends, based on their actions, personified the decaying bureaucracy. This segment of the government, due to hundreds of years of riches and power, had no or little accountability for their actions and thought themselves as entitled to do as they pleased. Clearly, power corrupts. If this axiom is accurate, from a political standpoint, it can be deduced that after many years of prosperity and power, they were morally corrupt, delusional and dangerous. As you note below, not only were they extremely dangerous, but their actions resulted in immensely destructive, irreparable ramifications to the nation.

History suggests the Doukases and their allies were incensed that the empress did not choose one of their own. They wanted the emperorship to remain with them or allies. They probably looked down at this upstart as inferior to them and due to erroneous perceptions, they probably believed it. But, on the contrary, as described by Norwich, among his attributes, Emperor Diogenes was intelligent, loyal, a brave soldier, courageous and competent. These encomiums are affirmed since prior to this battle, Romanus helped shore up military weakness of the previous administrations throughout their domains and strengthened the military.

His objective was to bring Byzantium back to its previous glory and protect its territories from intruders. He was aware of the rising Islamic threat principally presented by the Seljuk Turks who had recently concurred Armenia. In looking back, despite his many attributes, he had a glaring weakness; he was too trusting and did not know to what level of betrayal his enemies would go to, to gain power.

Prior to the battle, the king had a total of about thirty thousand soldiers with him. Sufficient to achieve victory. He decided that he would take fifteen thousand of the soldiers and confront the Seljuk army. He was going to lead the charge. He left Andronicus Doukas in charge of the remaining fifteen thousand with a directive—once the Seljuks have him surrounded, Andronicus was to charge and smash them. Had this strategy been followed, experts opined that it would have resulted in a Byzantine victory. Andronicus had no problem from the get-go to continue to express his dislike for the emperor. The reason, I assume, is they lost the power they previously held. And the new emperor was not one of them or their cronies. He was too honest and posed a serious risk to their personal goals.

The battle was long, and as expected, the Seljuk army surrounded the king and the fifteen thousand troops. Andronicus watched the battle from afar and did nothing. Once he saw the king fall to the ground, he said, "The emperor is dead," and took the remaining fifteen thousand troops back to Byzantium. In fact, Romanus was not dead and still fought on foot. Even when practically alone, he never left the fray and kept fighting, hoping for his soldiers' return. He was finally overcome. Doukas and the reserve soldiers, instead of joining and winning the battle for their king, went straight back to Constantinople. In fact, Andronicus raced back to the capital proclaiming another Doukas as the new emperor!

To his credit and class, Sultan Alp Arslan showed and treated Emperor Diogenes with respect. As the victor, he extracted a huge price to let him return to Constantinople. He wanted a significant amount of Anatolia and a sizeable amount of gold coins on an annual basis. The emperor had no choice but to agree. But fighting between the factions of Byzantium continued, and he never regained his throne. In fact, the new regime blinded him and blamed him for the loss. Blinding deposed emperors, apparently, was not rare in Byzantium deposed Emperors. And this good and courageous man was greatly abused and died shortly thereafter.

If the Doukases were wise, they would have complied with the terms agreed by Emperor Diogenis. They would have kept much of Anatolia. But they did not, and fighting continued on and off without success.

Bottom line, the loss of most of Anatolia to the Turks robbed Byzantium of their breadbasket and manpower. They never recovered from this loss that was orchestrated by the wealthy power-hungry bureaucrats. The castration of this nation hurt all, including the wrongdoers.

APPENDIX B

Garbis Family Tree

Garbis Family Tree

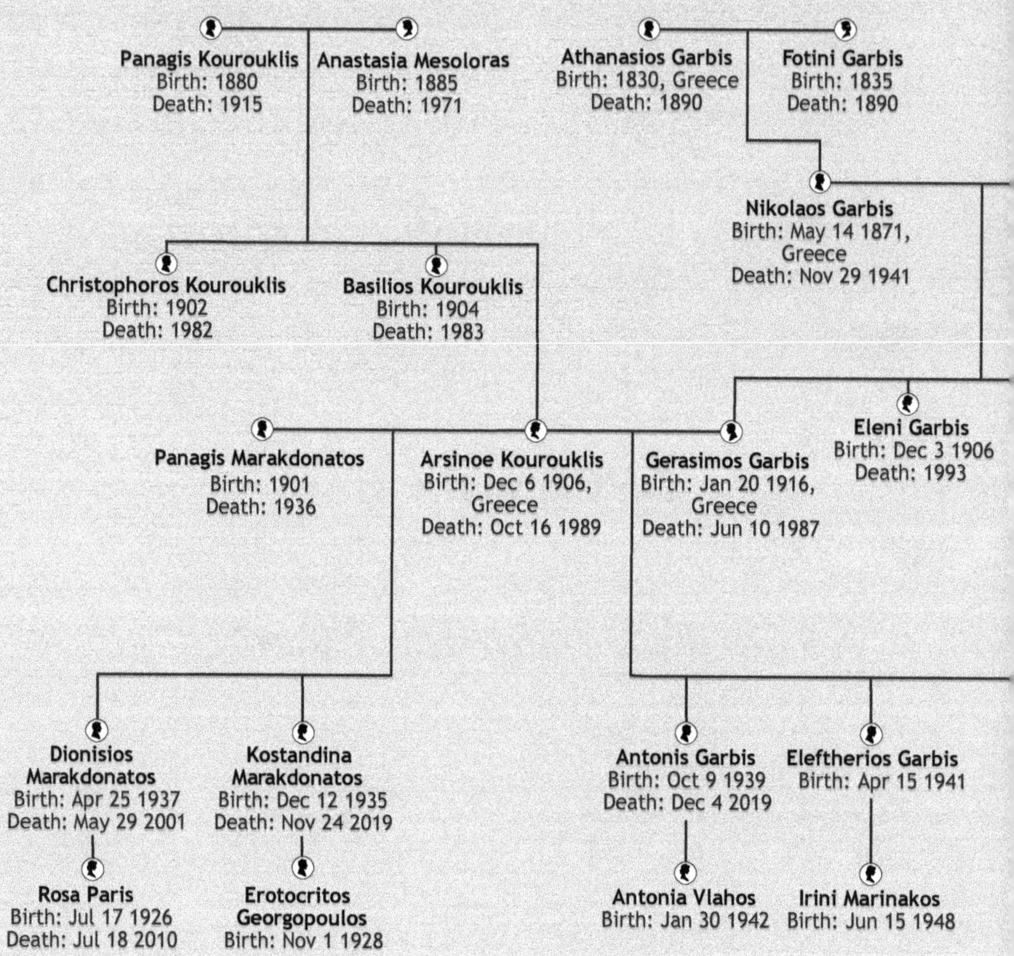

Panagis Kourouklis
Birth: 1880
Death: 1915

Anastasia Mesoloras
Birth: 1885
Death: 1971

Athanasios Garbis
Birth: 1830, Greece
Death: 1890

Fotini Garbis
Birth: 1835
Death: 1890

Nikolaos Garbis
Birth: May 14 1871, Greece
Death: Nov 29 1941

Christophoros Kourouklis
Birth: 1902
Death: 1982

Basilios Kourouklis
Birth: 1904
Death: 1983

Panagis Marakdonatos
Birth: 1901
Death: 1936

Arsinoe Kourouklis
Birth: Dec 6 1906, Greece
Death: Oct 16 1989

Gerasimos Garbis
Birth: Jan 20 1916, Greece
Death: Jun 10 1987

Eleni Garbis
Birth: Dec 3 1906
Death: 1993

Dionisios Marakdonatos
Birth: Apr 25 1937
Death: May 29 2001

Kostandina Marakdonatos
Birth: Dec 12 1935
Death: Nov 24 2019

Antonis Garbis
Birth: Oct 9 1939
Death: Dec 4 2019

Eleftherios Garbis
Birth: Apr 15 1941

Rosa Paris
Birth: Jul 17 1926
Death: Jul 18 2010

Erotocritos Georgopoulos
Birth: Nov 1 1928

Antonia Vlahos
Birth: Jan 30 1942

Irini Marinakos
Birth: Jun 15 1948

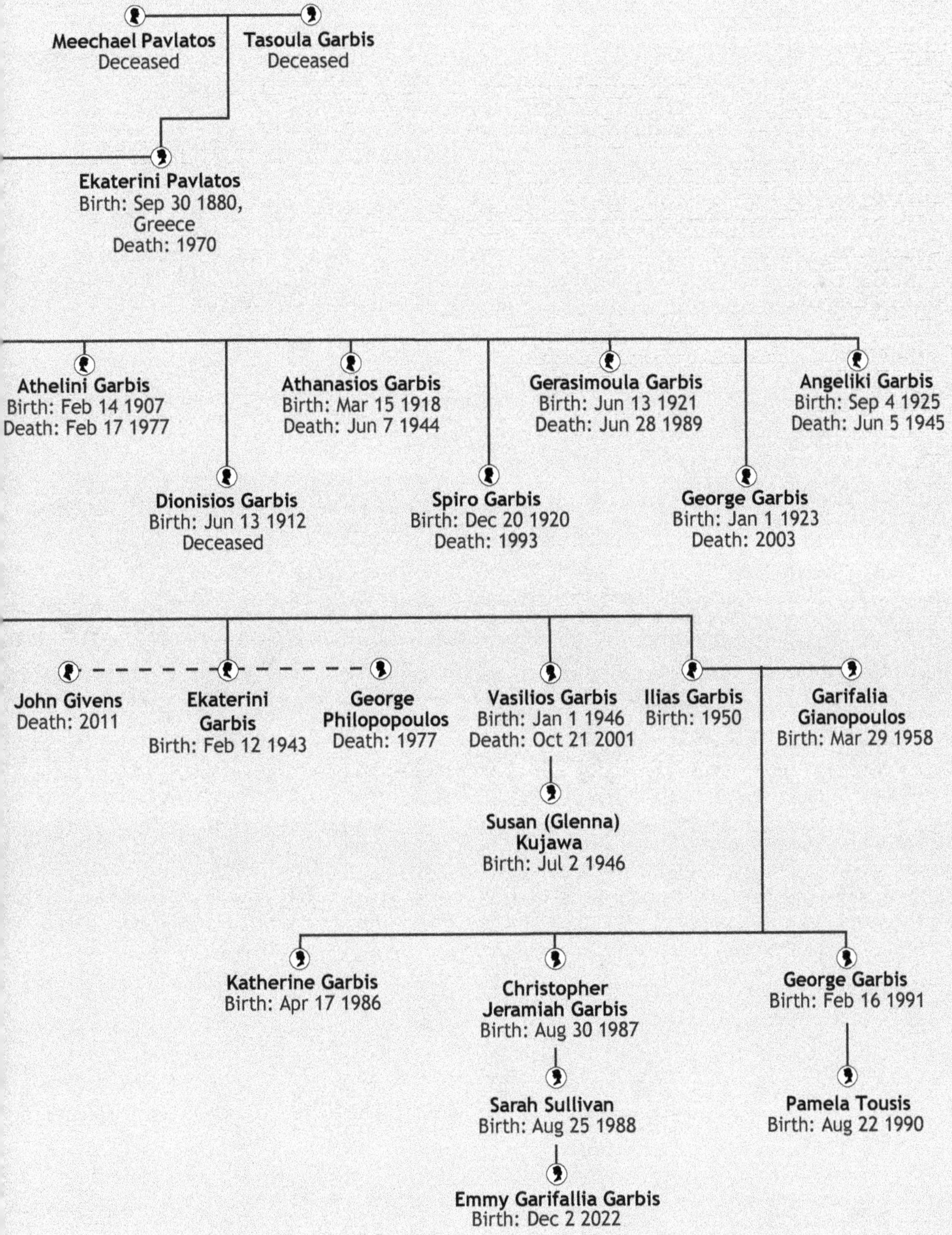

Garbis Family Tree

Meechael Pavlatos (Deceased) — **Tasoula Garbis** (Deceased)
└── **Ekaterini Pavlatos**
    Birth: Sep 30 1880, Greece
    Death: 1970

Children of Ekaterini Pavlatos:

- **Athelini Garbis** — Birth: Feb 14 1907; Death: Feb 17 1977
  - **Dionisios Garbis** — Birth: Jun 13 1912; Deceased
- **Athanasios Garbis** — Birth: Mar 15 1918; Death: Jun 7 1944
  - **Spiro Garbis** — Birth: Dec 20 1920; Death: 1993
- **Gerasimoula Garbis** — Birth: Jun 13 1921; Death: Jun 28 1989
  - **George Garbis** — Birth: Jan 1 1923; Death: 2003
- **Angeliki Garbis** — Birth: Sep 4 1925; Death: Jun 5 1945

Next generation:

- **John Givens** (Death: 2011) - - - **Ekaterini Garbis** (Birth: Feb 12 1943) — **George Philopopoulos** (Death: 1977)
- **Vasilios Garbis** — Birth: Jan 1 1946; Death: Oct 21 2001 — **Susan (Glenna) Kujawa** — Birth: Jul 2 1946
- **Ilias Garbis** — Birth: 1950 — **Garifalia Gianopoulos** — Birth: Mar 29 1958

Children:

- **Katherine Garbis** — Birth: Apr 17 1986
- **Christopher Jeramiah Garbis** — Birth: Aug 30 1987
  - **Sarah Sullivan** — Birth: Aug 25 1988
    - **Emmy Garifallia Garbis** — Birth: Dec 2 2022
- **George Garbis** — Birth: Feb 16 1991
  - **Pamela Tousis** — Birth: Aug 22 1990

APPENDIX C

Family Photos

From left to right, my brother Bill, Denny and me.

Left to right Uncle George, our Father in the navy and our Uncle Spiro. This was the beginning of WWII. Uncle Dionisios was already in Panama and Thanasi was in jail for Regina's death.

This the youngest brother of our father who unfortunately, killed his beloved. His name is Athanasios. Her name, Reggina.

Brother Bill when he was about seven

Brother Bill in his prime by some road near
the capital city, Argostoli.

The three amigos-brother Ted, our donkey Kapsulas and our best friend, Dickie.

Mother and Father at probably a family wedding.

Mother posing with our grandmother Athanasia.

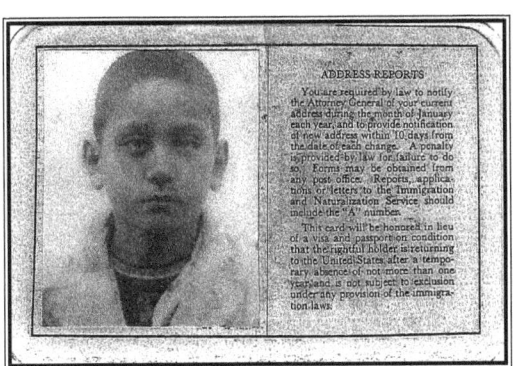

Me on my greencard when I entered the USA in August, 1958

Tony and Mom as we settled in Chicago.

Brother Denny probably soon after he arrived in Chicago.

My niece Stacy and her wonderful mom Rosie.

My uncle Spiro and wife Marianthi on their wedding day.

I incidentally found this photo when I was researching the devastation of the 1950 earthquake. Have no idea who the priest is but I am a fairly certain that the person next to him is my uncle George.

Left to right brother Tony, nephew Nick(?) being held by sister Dina, sister Kathy with our niece Kathy, our Mother and me. We are in front of our house.

This is the above house painted by a painter on the request of our brother Bill. Could not find a photograph. But it is a decent reflection of the actual house.

Of those I know from left to right standing: My grandmother Anastasia, Denny with left hand on young lady with scarf. Straight across from right to left is my mother, Olga, Olga's father and others I do not recall. Between Olga and mom is a youn Andoni. Sitting from right to left is me, Kathy and our young friends. next to Mom from left to right is me

My high school picture; Alumni of Oak Park High, 1969

Our wonderful mother, Tony and behind them is our nephew, Gus Markadonatos.

Brothers Denny and Bill. Both were very close.

Me, Denny, Phyllis, Susan and Dina.

This must have been on Kathy's marriage to John Givens. From left to right, Tony, Kathy, Denny, Bill, me a with the glasses and Ted.

Father, Mother and a great big brother.

All siblings before four passed: In the back, Bill, Ted, Denny and Kathy. Front, Tony, Dina and me.

Dina and Tony are sitting; me, Kathy and Ted are standing. Bill and Denny had passed.

Our father with our Peter, Stacy and Arsinoe. Our mother with Eva, Denny's and Roza's youngest.
The above photos were probably taken in the early 1960s.

Me saying an ethnic poem to commemorate the Greek revolution; which we celebrate as the Greek Independence Day-March 25, 18218-remember 400 pleads to remember the 400 years of occupation by the Turks.

Bill, our teacher(?) and me as you will note, photo was taken in 4/1959; about 7 months after arrival.

Our parents while visiting our sister Kathy and brother in law, George in Redondo Beach, California.

Phyllis and me after we were engaged. As you can see, I got really, REALLY lucky!

Family photo on Jeramiah's and Sarah's wedding day. The Church is St. Demetrios Church located by Church St. Elmhurst, IL.

Sarah and J in their Civil Wedding, that preceded the Church Wedding.

George and Pamela's wedding.

This is the holidays. Phyllis worked very hard and I hardly worked at all. But looking closely at the faces, you would never quess that I hardly worked!

Our oldest child and dearest-Katerina! She traveled to Europe in an excursion. This is at the Palace of Versailles, France.

Katerina with her best friend, and our best relative(:) Aubrie.

Jeramiah and Katerina going to Church.

Same as the above including Phyllis.

This is at the Biblical Gardens at Wisconsin Dales, Wisconsin. We would travel their annually until its closing.

Family in their teens. Left to right Jeramiah, George and Katherine celebrating K's Birthday at benihana, in Elmhurst? They loved mom. Dad, let's say, they tolerated.

Mom, Cousin John and Aunt Minoula. I believe this photo was taken in Greece.

Ted and Tony at liturgy at Stavromeny. Pasada, Kefalonia. This is an annual event. Ted and wife attend yearly. The reason for the picture is that I loved my mother so much, that I was willing to suffer embarrassment!

Left to right Grandmother Anastasia, Arsinoula, Dionisis, our beloved late Panagiotis, Stacy and our mother.

Our mother, arsinoula in Roza's arms, next to Roza looking up is me. Note the year.

Proud parents with their first child Katerina.

Proud father with the now grown up Katerina.

Louis and Phyllis Garbis; married on 9/26/1976

www.ingramcontent.com/pod-product-compliance
Lightning Source LLC
Chambersburg PA
CBHW061808070526
44586CB00024B/2758